BUTT FUMBLES,
FAKE SPIKES,
MUD BOWLS
& HEIDI GAMES

THE TOP 100 DEBACLES
OF THE

NEW YORK JETS

BUTT FUMBLES, FAKE SPIKES, MUD BOWLS & HEIDI GAMES

THE TOP 100 DEBACLES OF THE

NEW YORK JETS

BY
GREG PRATO

Written by Greg Prato
Printed and distributed by Greg Prato Writer, Corp
Published by Greg Prato Writer, Corp
Front cover design by Mary Prato
Interior photos by Greg Prato
Copyright © 2021, Greg Prato Writer, Corp. All rights reserved.
First Edition, August 2021

ISBN: 9798743654604

This book is dedicated to Brandon Moore's backside.

INTRODUCTION

At the time I assembled my 2011 book, *Sack Exchange: The Definitive Oral History of the 1980s New York Jets*, I was quite confident – as I'm sure many other fellow Jets fans were, as well – that Gang Green were in good hands with Rex Ryan and Mark Sanchez, and that the next step (after back-to-back trips to the AFC Championship Game) would be the Super Bowl/steady success.

A few months before the book's arrival, Ryan offered a memorable quote after the Jets shocked their rival, the New England Patriots, by beating them at Gillette Stadium in the Divisional Round – "'Same Old Jets,' going to the AFC Championship Game two years in a row." But almost as soon as that phrase left his lips, the team has offered up countless "Same Old Jets" moments *not* in a positive manner. In fact, between 2011-2020, they probably provided more undesirable "Same Old Jets" entries than any other 10-year period.

Out of all my years following the Jets, 2020 was most certainly one of their most excruciating seasons, as seemingly everything that could possibly go wrong, did (OK, OK…not *quite* as bad as Rich Kotite's swan song with the team, 1996, but still bloody awful). Which got me thinking about all the blunders and bloopers the team has provided its tormented fanbase post-Super Bowl III – quite a few of which I had the "pleasure" of watching unfold in real time.

Then it hit me – how about a book that listed and explained the 100 biggest Jets miscalculations over the years? You can say the famous saying, "Sometimes you have to laugh to keep from crying," played a big part in my decision to commit to such a project, and revisiting occurrences that I (and many Jets fans) wish never transpired.

So, won't you join me on a journey back through time – in which we can share a few laughs, and quite possibly, a few tears.

J-E-T-S! JETS! JETS! JETS!
Greg Prato

THE LIST

INCLUDED IN BACK OF BOOK
(as to not spoil all the surprises!)

100

The Jets Killed Carl

Larry David has a way of immortalizing sports figures (George Steinbrenner, Keith Hernandez, Bill Buckner, etc.) in shows that he's involved in. But how about immortalizing *an entire franchise*? In an episode entitled "The Ugly Section" in season 10 of *Curb Your Enthusiasm*, a golfing buddy of Larry's, named Carl, commits suicide. Why? He leaves a mysterious line in his suicide note, "I can't take any more disappointment," which Larry quickly deciphers. "That's what he used to say when we'd watch the Jet games together – 'I can't take any more disappointment!' That's an exact quote!" He then goes on to reflect, "I've seen that guy *sob* after losses. During games I've seen him sob. And they just kept losing and it kept eating at him and eating at him…and he couldn't take any more disappointment. The Jets killed Carl…*and a little bit of the Knicks.*"

99

A Skirmish at Studio 54

By 1983, disco was dead. But the former hotbed for partying and dancing the night away in the late '70s was still open for business, and continued to attract celebrities, including Jets Mark Gastineau and Ken O'Brien. But according to reports of what occurred on the evening of September 30, 1983 (two days after a loss to the Pats dropped the Jets to a record of 1-2), the pair wasn't in the mood for boogying, but rather, *brawling*.

The story goes that Gastineau and a bartender by the name of John Benson indulged in a game of arm-wrestling, Benson proved victorious, and before you knew it, tempers flared, and a fight ensued – which resulted in Benson and an onlooker sustaining broken noses. An assault complaint would be filed by Benson, which resulted in the case going to trial a year later, and Gastineau being found guilty of assault and O'Brien acquitted. On November 20th, Gastineau was sentenced to 90 hours of conducting football clinics at Rikers Island for prisoners between the ages of 16-21 (rather than a potential one-year jail term and a $1k fine).

Unfortunately, it seemed as though the Jets were feistier on the dancefloor than on the football field (offering disappointing records of 7-9 in both '83 and '84). This would not be the last time Gastineau found himself in trouble with the law, however (in 1993, he was sentenced to three years' probation for picking up a package of amphetamines at a Phoenix airport, and in 2000, was sentenced to 18 months in jail for not completing an anger management course, after a domestic violence incident).

98

Joe Namath...Actor?

No doubt, Joe Namath was a gifted athlete and one of the top sports personalities/celebrities of all-time. Heck, he was even a sought after TV pitchman for products (remember his now-classic Hanes Beautymist pantyhose commercial?).

But...could he act?

Some celebrity athletes have managed to carve out acting careers for themselves – Jim Brown, Arnold Schwarzenegger, Merlin Olsen, etc. And while Broadway Joe certainly tried to act in a few films in the early '70s – 1970's *Norwood* (a comedy with Glen Campbell and Dom DeLuise) and *CC and Company* (a biker flick with Ann-Margret), plus 1971's *The Last Rebel* (a western with Jack Elam) – let's just say he was most certainly *not* a thespian.

On the Rotten Tomatoes site, *CC and Company* currently holds a mere 22% audience score, while reviewers were none too kind concerning Broadway Joe's acting skills – Tony Mastroianni of the *Cleveland Press* said, "Football player Joe Namath should have stuck to football," while Gene Siskel of the *Chicago Tribune* said, "*CC and Company* is the film that asks the musical question, 'What do you want – bad acting or bad taste?'" Wisely, the Jets QB would not star in any further films during his playing days (although let's not forget his memorable cameo on the TV show, *The Brady Bunch*, in the 1973 episode, "Mail Order Hero" – in which Bobby Brady learns a valuable lesson concerning telling tall tales).

97

SNY Lets Ray Lucas Go

Post-game shows can be a real snoozer – usually former players pontificating far too much on the x's and o's, that soar over the head of the average/ordinary fan. But for quite a few seasons, ex-Jets QB Ray Lucas offered some colorful commentary and insight for *Jets Post Game Live* on SNY (a cable channel affiliated with the Mets, who would grant the Jets some airtime) that was not as one-dimensional as your average football talk show. In fact, since the Jets did not own the channel, the hosts of the post-game show were free to speak their mind if they didn't care for what they saw that day.

And when they teamed Lucas with Jonas Schwartz and another ex-Jet, Bart Scott, the show provided some much-needed relief – particularly during the dreary days of the Todd Bowles/Adam Gase eras. But in time for the 2020 season, Lucas was nowhere to be found. Why? It turns out it was due to monetary reasons, as Lucas failed to reach a deal on a new contract (and was replaced by another ex-Jet, Chad Cascadden).

But to his credit, Lucas couldn't have picked a better season to jump ship – Gase's horrific second (and thankfully, final) season as HC, in which the Jets farted out a 2-14 record. And Lucas even offered a perfect parting shot to his former employers, via a tweet during a game on September 20, 2020, in which the Jets would get slaughtered by the 49ers, 31-13, "Oh I forgot I'm not doing tv anymore so I don't have to watch this sh!t!!!"

96

Chad's Awkward Comments
to the Press

There is no denying the book smarts of ex-Jets QB Chad Pennington – finishing with a 3.83 grade point average while a student at Marshall and being a finalist for the Rhodes Scholarship. But he proved not all that wise concerning public speaking skills while addressing the media on December 20, 2004 – a day after the Jets beat the Seahawks, 37-14, while in the thick of a playoff race.

Something must have gotten under Pennington's skin concerning the reporters that covered his team, as he was quoted in the *New York Post* as saying, "You guys are privileged and honored to be a beat writer for the New York Jets…you have an opportunity to be around some of the greatest athletes in the world. That's an opportunity. It's not your right. It is a privilege."

I suppose the QB had overlooked the fact that at the time of his little scuffle with the press, the Jets were going on 35 years of a Super Bowl drought (which would unfortunately grow much longer…52 years and counting at the time of this book's release). Not to mention that the Jets would lose the remaining two games of the regular season after his tirade and would "back into" the playoffs that year.

Privilege, smivilege.

95

A Roughed Up Reporter

I admit, sports reporters can sometimes be downright obnoxious with their Mr. Know-It-All opinions (the phrase "Monday morning quarterback" immediately comes to mind concerning some of these foolers). But that said, it's not a good idea to physically rough up a reporter – which is what Jets QB Richard Todd did to *New York Post* writer Steve Serby back in 1981. Supposedly, Todd did not appreciate that Serby had been critical of him in the press – particularly when Serby implied that the Jets would be better off with the by-then-already-long-gone Matt Robinson as their QB. And as a result, there was tension between the two.

On November 5, 1981 (a few days after the Jets beat the Giants, 26-7, to bring their record to 4-4-1), a confrontation ensued between the QB and the reporter in the Jets locker room at the team's training center. Serby described in a *New York Post* article from 2015 that Todd "Grabbed me around the neck and smashed my head into a locker." Serby was treated afterwards at the Nassau University Medical Center (nearby to where the Jets practiced at the time, Hofstra University), and he and the paper filed criminal assault charges against the QB. Eventually, the Nassau County DA's office dismissed the criminal charges against Todd.

Todd only lasted two more seasons with the Jets, while Serby continues to write for the *Post* to this very day (2021).

94

Rex Ryan's Tattoo

It's not uncommon to get a tattoo pertaining to your favorite sports team on a part of your body. But it is not common for a head coach to get a tattoo relating to the team you're coaching at the time (for the simple fact that you never know how long your tenure with the team will last). And it is *super-duper* uncommon to get a tattoo of your wife (apparently bottomless, to boot) wearing the jersey of a specific player that you are currently coaching permanently etched into your skin. Especially, when that jersey (#6) is of a player who is far from "Hall of Fame caliber" – Mark "The Butt Fumbler" Sanchez.

But that is indeed what occurred at some point in late 2012/early 2013 – as the *Daily News* reported the story (complete with a photo of the tattoo on Ryan's right arm) on the back cover of their January 4, 2013 newspaper. And by 2015, after Ryan exited the Jets and signed on with the Buffalo Bills, he got the tat retouched so that the Jets green jersey was now replaced with Bills blue. It has never been confirmed if the #6 remained, but in case you were wondering, the Bills player sporting #6 at the time was punter Colton Schmidt.

But the real question is…did Rex regret the tattoo revision after being axed from the Bills after two unsuccessful seasons?

93

What a Thrilling Comeback Victory...Oops, Spoke Too Soon

The Jets enjoyed a bit of a revitalization in the late '70s – when they proved to be competitive and no longer a laughingstock, by posting two back-to-back .500 seasons (1978 and 1979), after three woeful campaigns (1975-1977, which saw them go 3-11 3x). And under the leadership of head coach Walt Michaels and a growing core of promising young players (led by Joe Klecko on defense and Wesley Walker on offense), things certainly seemed to be going in the right direction. And late in the '78 season, the Jets were actually still in the playoff hunt, but could not afford to lose...or be automatically eliminated.

And on December 10th, the Jets traveled to Cleveland to take on the Browns. Having seemingly sleepwalked through the first three quarters and finding themselves down 27-10, the Jets finally awoke and mounted an impressive comeback – not only tying the game late...but actually *going ahead by a touchdown* (on a run by RB Kevin Long), 34-27, with only 1:14 left on the clock. But the Browns and QB Brian Sipe refused to cry uncle – tying the game in regulation and winning it via a Don Cockroft field goal in OT...officially squashing the Jets' dream of a playoff berth.

The game also served as a maddening trait that the Jets would pull from their bag of tricks time and time again on future occasions –

mounting incredible comebacks against seemingly insurmountable odds to get their fans giddy with hope and potential euphoria, before delivering a painful shot to the private parts by losing late (the 1981 Wildcard and 2010 AFC Championship playoff games are the most glaring examples of this bad habit).

Final score: Browns 37, Jets 34.

92

A Touchdown Celebration That Stunk

Although it's hard to remember nowadays – since over-the-top player celebrations after any remotely meaningful play has become commonplace/expected in the NFL – there was a time that anything beyond spiking the ball in the end zone after a touchdown was unheard of. But by the late 2010's, NFL celebrating (and particularly, by NY teams) had regressed to the point of, well…*the toilet.*

Giants WR Odell Beckham imitated a dog lifting his leg and urinating after a touchdown in a game against the Eagles on September 24, 2017, and on September 20, 2018 against the Browns, Jets running back Isaiah Crowell upped the ante – by mimicking wiping his bottom with the football (before throwing the defiled object into the crowd). Expectedly, Crowell was flagged for unsportsmanlike conduct, publicly criticized by Jets HC Todd Bowles, and fined by the NFL (for $13,369).

But instead of recognizing his folly, Crowell was awarded an endorsement deal with a product called Dude Wipes, which is apparently a "toilet-paper substitute for men." However, there is a morale to the story. You may not want to work bathroom activities into your TD celebration – the Giants lost the aforementioned game, 27-24, and the Jets lost their game, 21-17, and both players would soon be gone from their respective NY teams after their controversial TD celebrations.

91

Hiring an Offensive Coordinator With Little Offensive Coordinating Experience

When you fire an offensive coordinator, it would make sense that the replacement should potentially be a clear improvement over the predecessor, right? Not so if you were the Jets circa 2012. There was no denying the football knowledge of the man they hired, Tony Sparano – he had been a college coach since 1984, and an NFL coach since 1999…heck, he was the *head coach* of the Dolphins from 2008-2011. But, he had been named "offensive coordinator" only one time in his career (back with Boston University, from 1989-1993).

Still, when the Jets parted ways with their OC, Brian Schottenheimer, after the 2011 season (who had been there since 2006), Sparano was hired as his replacement on January 11, 2012. Hmm. Perhaps Joe Namath summed it up best on ESPN's *The Michael Kay Show* the day after Sparano's hiring. "I am stumped," before adding, "I don't see it. I hope he's a great one, but I don't see it." Turns out that Broadway Joe *could* see something – the future. Sparano would only last as the Jets' OC for a single season (in which the Jets' offense finished 30th…*out of 32*) before getting axed.

90

NFL Player Strikes Ground
2 Jets Seasons

While you can make a valid argument that the 1982 NFL strike worked in the Jets' favor despite a shortened season (they finished 2nd in the AFC East and fell just short of Super Bowl XVII), there were two other instances in which work stoppages seemed to affect a Jets season negatively – 1975 and 1987.

Understandably, the early to mid '70s are a best forgotten era for the Jets, as they failed to construct a single winning season nor provide a single playoff appearance (not to mention head coaches coming and going, plus Joe Namath becoming older, injured, and brittle). But it is often forgotten that it appeared as though the Jets would be able to build on the strong finish of their 1974 regular season – winning six in a row to finish with a .500 record, after starting off with a putrid 1-7 mark – and hopefully, carry it over into '75.

However, when I spoke to former Jets center Joe Fields for the *Sack Exchange* book, he explained why things didn't go according to plan. "1975 started with a strike. We went on strike, and they let us back in on a Thursday. But there were only four teams that went out on strike – the Jets, the Patriots, the Redskins, and somebody else. Now, all the other teams kept practicing, and they let us back in on Thursday, and the season started on Sunday – we played Buffalo. We hadn't practiced in a whole week, and we ended up getting killed by Buffalo, 42-14. It wasn't a very good strike for us."

Indeed it wasn't. The Jets would finish the year with an awful 3-11 mark, and the stench would permeate throughout the next two seasons, as well (where they would match the same disappointing record in '76 and '77).

And there was a second time that this unfortunate chain reaction occurred. After the nightmarish ending to their 1986-87 season (see entries #37 and #8 for all the gory details), the Jets were seemingly back on the right track the following season – beating the Bills in week 1 (31-28) and the Pats the following week (43-24). And then…another players' strike occurred.

Instead of opting to cancel a portion of the season (a la '82), a single week was cancelled, before replacement players were enlisted to fill the void. Remember such names as David Norrie, John Chirico, or Tony Sweet? Me neither. But the Jets wound up going 1-2 during the three weeks they were utilizing fill-ins, until the regulars returned in time for week 7 (although at least one true Jet continued to play during the strike, Mark Gastineau).

Anyway, you could definitely make a valid argument that the strike upset the Jets' momentum – going 3-7 after the regulars returned, and missing the playoffs with a final 6-9 record.

89

Once Upon a Time, Playing In a Stadium Not Designed for Football

Shea Stadium was never a *true* football stadium. Watch just about any classic clip from the '60s or '70s of the Jets playing in this Flushing, Queens-based sports ground, and chances are, you will see footage of players trying to find their footing on dirt – rather than a full field of preferred green grass. And that is because they would be playing a top a baseball infield for portions of each season. From 1964-1983, the Jets shared their stadium with the New York Mets baseball team.

And as fans of America's National Pastime will know, the end of the baseball season overlaps with the beginning of football season. So, up until 1978, football games were not played in September at Shea *at all* – so that the playing field would not get too chewed up for the Mets. Why was it suddenly acceptable starting in '78 for the Jets to start playing home games in September?

Who the heck knows?

But in two instances – 1969 and 1973 – when the Mets had deep post-season runs that included trips to the World Series, the Jets did not play their first home games until even *later* than usual (October 20th in 1969, October 28th in 1973).

Also, since Shea was constructed apparently mostly with baseball in mind, the stadium was "open" behind where the outfield/bullpen was situated – which resulted in the Jets having to add makeshift bleachers in that area (whereas most football stadiums offered permanent/full 360 degree seating…which meant more seats = more potential $). Additionally, the Jets would enter and exit the field via the Mets' dugout.

So, all of these reasons contributed to what took place in entry #14 – much to the dismay of Jets fans (at least *Long Island-based* Jets fans).

88

Lou Holtz's Not Quite Full Season's Fight Song

While America was celebrating 200 years of independence in 1976, the Jets were celebrating…well, *nothing*. How bad were the Jets in 1976? They were nearly "2020 bad" – going 3-11 during Joe Namath's final season with the Jets. Entering America's Bicentennial year, the Jets had a new head coach in place – Lou Holtz (having replaced interim coach Ken Shipp, who was filling in for the recently-fired Charley Winner). And Holtz's resume as a college head coach at North Carolina State University was impressive – compiling a 33-12-3 record in four seasons and winning the ACC Championship in 1973. So, what the heck – why not give him a shot, right?

In Lou Holtz's sole season as "HC of the NYJ" (oops…wrong entry for that abbreviation!), the Jets made an artform out of getting blown out on a regular basis – with the worst keyster-kickings occurring vs. the Broncos (46-3 in week 2), the Pats (41-7 in week 6), the Bengals (42-3 in week 14)…do we need to continue? However, it's very rare for a newly-appointed head coach to not finish at least one whole season (heck, Rich Kotite and Adam Gase somehow completed *two* full seasons each).

With one game remaining on the schedule, rumors began to swirl that Holtz would soon be exiting. Jets running back, Clark Gaines, explained in *Sack Exchange* what happened next. "I do remember Lou telling us at the very last meeting, 'Gentlemen, I came here with you, and I will be here with you. So you can count on that.' The next day, they call a hasty meeting before the normal session. Mike Holovak walks in the room – no Lou Holtz – and he says, 'Gentlemen, I will be your interim coach for the rest of the year'."

It turns out that Holtz just wasn't cut out for coaching in the NFL, but was indeed better suited for college football – in the wake of his Jets fiasco, he coached four college teams (Arkansas, Minnesota, Notre Dame, and South Carolina) between 1977-2004, won the 1988 Fiesta Bowl with the Fighting Irish, and was inducted into the College Football Hall of Fame in 2008.

However, it turns out that Holtz's Jets legacy contains one more nugget that deserves mention. It's a forgone conclusion that many football players do *not* have sweet singing voices ("Superbowl Shuffle," anyone?). So, why Holtz would force his team to sing a "Fight Song" during his one-and-only truncated season as the Jets HC remains another befuddling moment in the franchise's history.

The team was instructed to sing the tune (composed by Mr. Holtz) after every win, and the lyrics went something like this – "When the game acts like men, we're together win or lose, New York Jets keep rolling along. And where we go, we'll let the critics know, that the Jets are here to stay!"

Oy vey.

87

Leon's Secret to Success

For some, moving one's bowels is a highpoint of the morning, afternoon, or evening. But should it be declared in a global sports publication? In the June 29, 2009 issue of *ESPN The Magazine* (with Russian tennis player Maria Sharapova on the cover), Jets running back/return specialist Leon Washington opened the lid on his secret to success (there were multiple entries throughout the issue that featured various athletes answering what "my secret" was).

"After we warm up before a game, I gotta take a dump. It's a huge benefit to release that gas you don't need. The facilities are beautiful. We're spoiled. If I get a good one, I know I am gonna score two touchdowns."

Turns out that Washington did a good job of releasing gas he didn't need throughout his career – as of this book's release, he is tied with Josh Cribbs and Cordarrelle Patterson for most kickoff return touchdowns in NFL history (with eight). Some may say it's ironic that in a book comprised of Jets failures, there is an entry about success.

Either way, the situation didn't totally stink.

86

Well, At Least We Have Jay Fiedler as a Back-up QB... Oh Wait, We Don't

Chad Pennington at full strength was certainly a talented NFL QB. But one small problem – he had one heck of a time remaining healthy and staying on the gridiron for extended lengths of time. Learning from past blunders when it came to having below-par back-up QB's on their roster, the Jets signed former Dolphins starting QB (and NY native) Jay Fiedler as their "insurance" for the 2005 season.

And during the third game of the season against the Jaguars (a game they would lose in OT, 26-20), Pennington tore the rotator cuff in his right shoulder (for the second time in his career) – which led to the immediate end of his season, and Fiedler getting the damn ball.

Unfortunately, the "Fiedler era" of the Jets was fleeting – a total of *seven plays*, to be exact – before he dislocated his right shoulder, and eventually had to undergo arthroscopic surgery, ending *his* season, as well. With both QB's down, the Jets enlisted the "aid" of Brooks Bollinger, Kliff Kingsbury, and an over-the-hill Vinny Testaverde – resulting in a dreadful 4-12 record.

85

Titans Throwback Helmets/ Uniforms Rather Than '78-'97 Jets Helmets/Uniforms

For Jets fans like myself who started following the team in the early '80s, the all-green helmets with the JETS logo in white were pretty darn cool-looking – sleek, stylish, and snazzy. But understandably, since the team mostly stunk to high heaven while sporting that styled helmet, when Bill Parcells suggested a return to the Namath-era looking helmet in 1998, it made sense.

However, with NFL teams starting to regularly bring back "throwback" helmets and uniforms in the early 21st century for a few games per season, the Jets would opt to revive the blah-looking navy blue and gold helmets/unis of their pre-Jets "New York Titans" days.

And this would have been a golden opportunity to pay tribute to the '80s era of the Sack Exchange, Wesley Walker, Freeman McNeil, Ken O'Brien, and Al Toon, by having the Jets return to their '80s look for a game or two. But for reasons unknown, the higher ups would rather pay tribute to such legendary players as Bob Scrabis, Thurlow Cooper, and Laverne Torczon.

Who? *Exactly*.

84

Washington Jetskins

It's not uncommon for a team to model their roster after a Super Bowl winning team. But it's not all that common to poach four players from the same team – a team that never rose above "pretty good" status. But that's exactly what the Washington Redskins did in 2003, when they were often referred to in the press as the "Washington Jetskins," when four free agents – wide receiver Laveranues Coles, kick returner Chad Morton, guard Randy Thomas, and kicker John Hall – all skedaddled from NY to DC.

Was it all worth it? No. It wasn't. The Redskins would wind up going 5-11, while the Jets – who were obviously weakened by losing key players like Coles (who had developed a strong chemistry with QB Chad Pennington in 2002) – would end up going 6-10. And the former Jets they acquired didn't turn out to be long-term acquisitions – in fact, the Redskins would trade Coles back to the Jets after just two seasons. But the Redskins *can* say they beat the Jets in week 1 that season, 16-13.

So at least they had that going for them.

83

Tebow Time

Perhaps the Jets were still a bit too mesmerized by what they had witnessed first-hand on the evening of November 17, 2011, when they lost a tight one to the Broncos at Sports Authority Field at Mile High – when Denver's unconventional QB, Tim Tebow, single-handedly beat Gang Green late in the game, 17-13 (a winnable game that later would prove crucial to the outcome of the Jets' season, when they missed the playoffs by a single win).

With Tebow already a certified celebrity after winning the Heisman Trophy in 2007, penning the popular book *Through My Eyes* (more than one million copies sold!), and then leading the Broncos to the playoffs in 2011, he was put on the trading block by Denver after they signed Peyton Manning in the off-season.

Instead of the Jets looking for a veteran QB to help mentor Mark Sanchez (who experienced some major developmental difficulties in his third pro season) and who could serve as a serviceable QB if their starter faltered or got injured, they worked out a trade with Denver (the Jets gave up fourth and sixth-round draft picks) on March 21, 2012, in which Tebow would be their second stringer.

What resulted was a situation that was never made completely clear if Tebow was supposed to be primarily used on special teams, in the offense as part of wildcat formations, or as a QB. The result was Tebow barely being used, and the media and fans alike calling for him to start over Sanchez at various points (since #6 struggled mightily that season, once again).

Tebow was never given a fair chance to show what he could do (throwing only 8 passes and rushing 32 times the entire season, of which he was injured for several games) – and after the Jets' lousy 2012 season ground to a halt, in which they finished a disappointing 6-10 – Tebow was released by the team.

82

The Jamal Adams Saga

During the bleak Todd Bowles/Adam Gase eras, for a few of those years (2017-2019), at least Jets fans could find some solace in the fact that their team featured one of the game's best young players in strong safety Jamal Adams. Being named All-Pro (2019), playing in two Pro Bowls (2018 and 2019, and being named "Defensive MVP" in the first one), and coming in at #27 in the NFL Top 100 Players of 2020 poll (voted on by fellow football players), Adams was clearly the Jets' top defensive player since the heady days of when Darrelle Revis regularly shut down opposing receivers as a cornerback.

Going into the 2020 season, Adams figured he was worth a long-term contract. The higher ups thought not. Hence, Adams was gone with the wind. On July 25, 2020, the Jets sent Adams and a 2022 fourth-round pick to the Seahawks, in exchange for two first-round picks (2021 and 2022), a third-round pick (2021), plus safety Bradley McDougald. After the trade, Adams would be named to his third straight Pro Bowl, while the Jets were gruesomely "Gase'd" – going 2-14.

81

The Jets' Worst
Regular Season Loss Ever?

The Jets have endured some truly unsightly losses during the regular season (the Fake Spike Game, the Butt Fumble Game, the 2015 "win and get in" game vs. the Bills, etc.). But one of the worst losses – from a score standpoint – will forever belong to a best-forgotten game in 1979. Coming off a hard luck loss in the season opener vs. the Browns at Shea, 25-22 in OT (the amount of painful losses the Jets suffered at the hands of the Browns during the '70s/'80s was quite overwhelming, eh?), the Jets showed up at Schaefer Stadium on September 9th, for a week 2 match-up vs. division rivals the Pats.

Well, if Gang Green never even bothered to get off the team bus, the score wouldn't have been much worse. On that ominous day, Pats QB Steve Grogan passed for 315 yards and 5 touchdowns (the latter a long-standing club record, until Tom Brady shattered it in 2007 with 6) and the team gained 597 yards. Meanwhile, the Jets coughed up 3 fumbles, allowed a total of 9 sacks, lobbed 3 interceptions, and for good measure, endured 1 blocked punt.

Jets HC Walt Michaels succinctly summed up the effort (or more fittingly, *lack* of effort) by his team to *The New York Times* – "No excuse. They are grown men. They work for a living. They get paid. It was a halfhearted effort, and it wasn't individuals. It was all 45."

Final score: Patriots 56, Jets 3.

80

Billy "White Shoes" Johnson

Wide receiver/return specialist Billy "White Shoes" Johnson (take a wild guess how he earned his nickname) was certainly a talented football player. Most importantly, entering the College Football Hall of Fame in 1996 (he attended Widener College in Pennsylvania), and being named to 3 Pro Bowls during his 16 year pro career (which included stints with the Houston Oilers, the Montreal Alouettes of the CFL, the Atlanta Falcons, and the Washington Redskins), among other accolades.

But let's be honest…in an era rich with big-name NFL talent (Joe Montana, Lawrence Taylor, Walter Payton, etc.), he was *not* exactly a player that many would have figured to transform into a one-man wrecking crew. Well, on the afternoon of October 23, 1983 as a member of the Falcons, the wide receiver/return specialist did just that against the Jets.

With the Jets entering the game with a 3-4 record (having lost two straight) and the Falcons with a 2-5 record (having lost four straight), it appeared as though the Jets were finally back on track late in the game – blowing out the Falcons 21-0, as the 3rd quarter was winding down. And then…"White Shoes" went to work. With just four seconds remaining in the quarter, Falcons QB Steve Bartkowski connected with Johnson for a 25-yard TD, to make it 21-7.

Then within a minute and 44 seconds, Johnson provided the Falcons with a pair of outstanding punt returns – the first for 41 yards (which set up his team nicely at the Jets' 25-yard line, resulting in a TD from Bartkowski to RB William Andrews), followed by returning a punt 71 yards for a TD, to tie the game at 21. The Falcons then went ahead with a pair of field goals by Mick Luckhurst, while the Jets' offense completely dozed off in the final quarter and did not score another point.

The loss exposed the Jets as pretenders rather than contenders in '83 – going on to finish 7-9 and missing the playoffs for the first time in three years (and finishing last in the AFC East), while the Falcons could do no better (finishing last with the same record in the NFC West). But thanks to his unforgettable performance one rainy autumn afternoon at Shea in 1983, the name "Billy 'White Shoes' Johnson" will live on forever amongst frustrated Jets fans.

Final score: Falcons 27, Jets 21.

79

Shouldn't They Be Called the New Jersey Jets?

When Jets fans were met with the unpleasant news that the Jets were fleeing Flushing for East Rutherford (and to make matters worse, would be co-inhabiting a venue named *Giants* Stadium), some figured the New York Jets would be rechristened the New Jersey Jets. Heck, even during the Jets' last-ever game at Shea – a 34-7 ass-kicking administered by the Pittsburgh Steelers, on December 10, 1983 – the smarty-pants scoreboard operator briefly switched "NY Jets" to "NJ Jets" at one point during the game.

But by the time the Jets began the '84 season in their new home, it was clear that they had opted to stick with the New York Jets name (despite the whole reason why they were called "the Jets" in the first place was because of noisy aircrafts from nearby LaGuardia Airport continuously flying over *Shea*).

But…if a team is no longer playing in NY state, why the heck should they keep the "NY" in their name? It turns out that the short-lived USFL team the New Jersey Generals (who *also* played in Giants Stadium!) was the only team with the cajones big enough to actually go with NJ over NY – something that both the Jets and Giants were apparently too skittish about committing to.

Of course, the answer was obvious – it all came down to dollars and cents, and having "New York" as part of your name will obviously bring in a whole heck of a lot more revenue than "New

Jersey" (and by keeping it "NY," fans still disappointed about the move could at least cling on to that last tiny morsel of goodwill).

Admittedly though, the "Jersey Jets" would have had a nice ring to it...

78

Free Agency and Draft Navigator Gets Fired a Few Weeks Later

There are many reasons why a general manager of an NFL team can get fired. But probably the most common would be if their team consistently loses, if they draft poorly, and/or sign the wrong free agents. So, from those standpoints, Jets GM Mike Maccagnan scored an undesirable hat trick – and certainly deserved to be relieved of his duties. After all, during his four seasons as GM (2015-2018), the Jets constructed a terrible 24-40 record with not a single invite into the playoffs, signed many a free agent failure (Darrelle Revis, Isaiah Crowell, Spencer Long, etc.), and selected many a draft disappointment (Christian Hackenberg, Darron Lee, Sam Darnold, etc.).

A cleaning of house was definitely in order after the Jets' 2018 season was put out of its misery (after going 4-12), and on December 30, 2018, HC Todd Bowles was fired – as expected. But unexpectedly, it was announced that Maccagnan would be retaining his job. So, there he remained – spotted sitting alongside Jets CEO Christopher Johnson and newly signed HC Adam Gase at Gase's introductory press conference on January 14, 2019, and also, put in charge of the upcoming draft and the signing of free agents.

And which free agents did he sign? One certified bust (Le'Veon Bell, who would be off the Jets a little over one season later), and one probable bust at the time of this book's arrival (C.J. Mosley, who played only two games due to injury in 2019, then opted to sit out 2020 due to the COVID pandemic).

So, on April 25th, Maccagnan oversaw the Jets' draft, selecting DT Quinnen Williams, OLB Jachai Polite, OT Chuma Edoga, and TE Trevon Wesco. But then, on May 15th (no, your eyes don't deceive you – less than *a month* after the draft took place), Maccagnan was fired from the Jets and eventually replaced by Joe Douglas.

Why wasn't he fired during the 2018 season or immediately after alongside Bowles? Who the heck knows for sure. But his eventual ousting was later attributed in the press to a power struggle with Gase, and/or Johnson supposedly not being happy with Maccagnan's handling of the draft. Either way, in true Jets style, Maccagnan was allowed to provide a major say-so in the Jets' future just before being fired.

Makes sense? Of course it doesn't.

77

A Mid-Game Weiner

It's understandable for professional sports players to work up an appetite during a game. After all, nerves probably prevent eating a 7 course meal before a game, not to mention all the calorie burning involved during a contest. But in this day and age with athletes obsessed with proper nutrition, it would probably be a rarity for a pro quarterback to eat a frankfurter. But what about…eating one during a game, *on the sideline*? However far-fetched this may sound; it did happen at least one time in NFL history – and a New York Jet was the culprit.

During a week 7 game on October 25, 2009, in which the Jets were destroying the Raiders in Oakland (*a rarity*) – the final score would be 38-0 – with only minutes remaining in the game, a TV camera spotted Sanchez chowing down on a hot dog, while sitting on the sideline. Sanchez later apologized for letting his stomach rule his mind, and did a good deed shortly thereafter – purchasing 500 hot dogs and 500 hamburgers (along with buns and rolls) and donating them to the Community Soup Kitchen of Morristown, New Jersey.

76

De-feet

What consenting adults choose to do in the romance department behind closed doors – *as long as they're not harming anyone nor breaking the law* – is their own business. But in the internet/media-crazed day and age of the early 21st century, countless videos were uploaded for the public to inspect that the "creators" possibly later regretted. Case in point, when Rex Ryan's wife, Michelle, allegedly uploaded a series of goofy foot fetish videos online.

On December 21, 2010, the Deadspin site posted an article under the headline "This May Or May Not Be Rex Ryan's Wife Making Foot-Fetish Videos." In the article, it mentioned how a few years back, a YouTube user going by the name of "ihaveprettyfeet" had posted several videos, in which she would display her feet, for all to see. Although there was nothing pornographic included in the videos (YouTube doesn't allow "adult content" videos to be posted on their site), the account was eventually banned – before other YouTubers began reposting the videos.

And with Rex's celebrity profile obviously heightened as the head coach of the Jets, when one of these videos purportedly featuring Michelle sticking her bare feet outside a car window and a gent off-camera providing dialogue that sounded an awful like her husband's voice (remarking "They are beautiful," and after touching them, that "They are like, *really* soft"), the aforementioned Deadspin article was assembled. And the article featured not only that video clip, but several others featuring a woman who certainly resembled Michelle Ryan. As expected, this story was picked up by many news outlets – with the Jets in the midst of a battle for a playoff spot in late December, when off-field distractions are the last thing a contending team wants.

And although they did lose their next game (38-34 against the Bears), this diversion shockingly did *not* lead to a late-season swoon – the Jets actually made the playoffs, anyway (even prior to winning the last game of the season vs. the Bills, 38-7) and eventually reaching the AFC Championship Game.

But as it turns out, the largely motor-mouthed Rex suddenly clammed up about the story behind this video footage at a press conference. When asked, he replied, "To be honest, and I get it, I know you need to ask and all that stuff. But it's a personal matter and I'm really not going to discuss it, OK?"

OK, Sexy Rexy.

75

Author Rex

It seems like most pro-sports head coaches wait to write a book until *after* they've won at least one championship as the leader of their team. In 2011, Rex Ryan apparently couldn't wait any longer, and Doubleday Books released *Play Like You Mean It: Passion, Laughs, and Leadership in the World's Most Beautiful Game.* Admittedly, at this point, the Jets were coming off back-to-back AFC Championship Game appearances (in what just happened to be Ryan's first two seasons as HC of the Jets), and the immediate future looked bright, so you can kind of see Doubleday's interest in putting out such a book.

But if Ryan was so confident that he didn't "intend to kiss Bill Belichick's rings" or "I think we'll get to meet him [then-US president Barack Obama] in the next couple of years, anyway" (two memorable quotes from the introductory press conference of his hiring) then shouldn't he have waited to pen a book until *after* winning a Super Bowl with the Jets?

Actually, on second thought, it's best that he wrote this book (which is awfully full of self-congratulations and patting oneself on the back) when he did, because after his second year as the Jets' HC, the team got worse and worse. Forget not reaching the Super Bowl, they never again even reached *the playoffs* with Ryan at the helm (before he got the axe in 2014). And if you wanted to read about Rex coming clean concerning his wife's alleged foot fetish videos, the Inés Sainz incident, or the "Human Wall," forget it – he refused to dig deep and offer any major revelations concerning the tougher subjects.

But, if you'd like to read subsequently humorous blowhard-ian statements and viewpoints, then you're in luck – including a claim that the Jets were better than the Giants. "Some people like to say the Giants are the big brother team and the Jets are the little brother team. I know it's going to piss off every Giants fan to hear this, but here you go: I really don't care. We came to New York City to be the best team in the NFL, not just the best team in New York City. And I have news for you: We are the better team. We're the big brother."

Of course, just a few months after this brash declaration, the Giants beat the Jets in the second to last game of the season (more on this in entry #71) – which served as a launching pad for Big Blue to win Super Bowl XLVI over the Patriots.

And what about him gushing the following glowing remarks about Mark Sanchez: "He's the real deal. He has all the intangibles: talent, charisma, intellect, and leadership abilities. I believe Mark's going to be extraordinary in the NFL."

Boy, Rex sure didn't seem all that enamored with Mark when he inserted him in a meaningless preseason game that resulted in a season-ending – and subsequently, Jets career-ending – injury in 2013 (see entry #47).

Want another nugget? I saved the best for last. "The bottom line for me and the Jets is, we'll get there. We're right there now, and everybody knows it. That's why I don't back down when people ask if we're going to win the Super Bowl. The answer is yes. We're going to do it."

That Rex was quite a jolly/fun fellow, wasn't he?

74

Author Keyshawn

It makes most sense for players to wait until *after* their playing days are over to write a book chronicling the ups and downs of their careers – to prevent rubbing your teammates and those closely connected to the team (and working alongside you) the wrong way. Not Keyshawn Johnson. In his 1997 book, *Just Give Me the Damn Ball!: The Fast Times and Hard Knocks of an NFL Rookie*, Johnson referred to underdog (and widely beloved) Jets receiver Wayne Chrebet as the coach's "mascot," "pet," and "the little dude from Hofstra," as well as a player that "wouldn't even make anybody else's team."

And the motor-mouthed Johnson didn't stop there! Jets quarterback Neil O'Donnell also felt his wrath (calling him "a stiff puppet"), as well as offensive coordinator Ron Erhardt (who he deemed "an old fool"). However, the book (which Keyshawn dedicated to four people – Jesus Christ, his mother, his daughter, and…himself) didn't prove to be toxic to the team – it was later reported that newly-appointed Jets head coach Bill Parcells had arranged for Johnson and Chrebet to have lockers side by side (to defuse any potential ill will), while O'Donnell stated he and the wide receiver had "no problem at all" and had been weightlifting together.

73

Replay Officials Suffer
a Brain Fart

Shortly after Bill Belichick and Tom Brady transformed the Patriots into the Evil Empire and began dominating the league year after year after year, it seemed as though the referees and replay officials had gone gaga over the aforementioned dynamic duo. So much so, that it appeared as though endless close calls always seemed to go in the Pats' favor. And perhaps the most preposterous of these "Pats far-fetched calls" occurred against (who else?) the Jets, on October 15, 2017.

In an important game versus the Pats in week 6 (the Jets were standing at 3-2 at the time, after 3 consecutive wins), the Jets blew an early 14-0 lead, and wound up down 24-14 in the 4th quarter. But with 8:31 remaining in the game, Jets tight end Austin Seferian-Jenkins appeared to haul in a four-yard touchdown catch from QB Josh McCown – which would have (with a successful extra point) brought the score differential down to a mere field goal, with plenty of time left.

However, ecstasy soon turned to agony, as the refs overturned the call after a review and ruled that Seferian-Jenkins had fumbled the ball out of the end zone for a touchback.

Huh?

Replays showed that it looked like Seferian-Jenkins did indeed score…but apparently, the "replay experts" in Manhattan must have wanted to get back to watching re-runs of *Gilligan's Island*, because of course, the call ultimately went the Pats' way, who wound up winning by (take a guess) *a touchdown*.

And instead of an important division win for the Jets, it was a heartbreaking loss (even later mentioned in the aforementioned *Curb Your Enthusiasm* episode, "The Ugly Section") – which led to the usual annual Jets' season spiral, as they lost eight of their next ten games.

Thank you, replay officials.

Final score: Patriots 24, Jets 17.

72

West Side Stadium

Since 1984, the Jets had called Giants Stadium their home (although the team and its fans liked to refer to it as "The Meadowlands" rather than "Giants Stadium"…guess the truth hurt, eh?), located in East Rutherford, New Jersey. So whether they wanted to admit it or not, the Jets and their fans – deep down inside – would have preferred to have their own stadium, *in New York*. In the early 21st century, it was proposed that a stadium with a retractable roof could be constructed on the west side of Manhattan – built on a platform over rail yards (close to the Hudson River).

The only catch is that it would be one heck of a financial undertaking (the construction cost was going to be *over $1 billion*) – and would require public financing. However, the Jets offered to pay for the majority of the cost…if the city and state was willing to provide $250 million to construct the platform.

Not to mention, there would be no large parking space near the stadium – so fans' pre-game/post-game get-togethers were out of the question. But in addition to the Jets calling the stadium their home, it was disclosed that it would also host Super Bowl XLIV in 2010 (eventually going to Miami), and also, part of New York's bid for the 2012 Summer Olympics (eventually going to London).

However, it all fell through after it was met by intense opposition by seemingly most of the locals (due to the additional traffic congestion it would cause whenever events would be held there) and most visibly, Cablevision (who owned Madison Square

Garden) – who launched a campaign that opposed the stadium. Eventually, a vote of three state representatives (New York State Assembly Speaker Sheldon Silver, New York State Senate Majority Leader Joseph Bruno, and New York Governor George Pataki) was conducted to determine the fate of the West Side Stadium…which was ultimately, vetoed.

So, instead of getting their own stadium, the Jets were once again co-tenants with their big brothers, the Giants, at the eventually christened MetLife Stadium, constructed right next to where the old Giants Stadium once stood (and opened in 2010).

71

Awakening Sleeping Giants

With two games to go in the 2011 season, the Jets just needed to probably win one to clinch a playoff spot for the third year in a row (the first time such a feat would ever occur in the franchise's history). And on Christmas Eve, the Jets were primed to give their fans an early holiday gift – by beating the team they share MetLife Stadium with, the Giants.

However, instead of putting all of his efforts into focusing on the task at hand, Rex Ryan decided to pull a fast one, and put black curtains over the four painted Super Bowl logos (representing each time Big Blue appeared in the SB up to that point) outside the teams' locker rooms prior to the game for reasons unknown. If anything, the Jets actually *seeing* the tribute to the Giants' SB appearances may have inspired the team to aim high and show their stadium co-tenants that they were to be taken seriously.

Instead, it became later known in the press that several Giants players took this blatant "cover up" as a sign of disrespect – which may have served as inspiration to the Giants' subsequent manhandling of the Jets, 29-14. The undisputed highlight – or more fittingly *lowlight*, if you're a Jets fan – was Giants WR Victor Cruz scoring on a 99-yard play to give the Giants a 10-7 lead (a lead that they would never relinquish) in the 2nd quarter, capped off by Cruz's trademark "salsa dance" in the end zone.

Quite possibly, you could make a valid argument that the Jets' show of poor etiquette served as a lightning rod for the Giants –

they would go on to not lose a single game the rest of the way, including beating the Patriots in Super Bowl XLVI. The Jets? They would go on to lose their final game to the Dolphins, 19-17 (fully examined in the next entry), and miss the playoffs entirely.

Final score: Giants 29, Jets 14.

70

Hissy Fit In the Huddle

Understandably, tensions can run high among professional sports players – especially if it's the last game of the NFL regular season, and your team is trying to avoid being denied a ticket to the playoffs. Which is the exact predicament the Jets found themselves in on New Year's Day 2012.

With the Jets trailing 19-10 and the end of the game fast approaching (at the two-minute warning, to be precise), Jets wide receiver Santonio Holmes had a temper tantrum and began arguing with offensive tackle Wayne Hunter – resulting in Holmes being astonishingly yanked out of the huddle and replaced by Patrick Turner, as the Jets tried to rally. Holmes would not play another down that game.

And although the Jets did manage to squeeze in a TD to make it 19-17, an onside kick attempt was not successful, and the Jets kissed their playoff chances goodbye – while Holmes (who was also one of the team's captains) watched from the sideline.

A team source would tell ESPN NFL Insider Adam Schefter that Holmes had "quit" on the team during those last two minutes, with Jets RB LaDainian Tomlinson quoted as saying, "It's tough for guys to follow a captain that kind of behaves in that manner. You've got to lead by example, and you've got to play your tail off until the last play."

And while it was said in the press that it was the "coach's call" to bench Holmes (who would only last one more season with the Jets, and be out of football all together after 2014), to add some more absurdity into the mix, Rex Ryan later admitted that he thought it was Holmes who took *himself* out. So the question remains…who told who to sit out?

Eh, who cares.

Final score: Dolphins 19, Jets 17.

69

Let's Hire My Son-in-Law as My Replacement

You have a talented defensive coordinator, Walt Michaels, waiting in the wings (who oversaw a defense that shut down the big bad Baltimore Colts in Super Bowl III) to become your replacement as Jets head coach when you decide the time has come to step down. It should have been a no-brainer for Weeb Ewbank to "hand the ball off" to Michaels when he chose to retire in 1972. But…this is the Jets, so of course, no. Instead, Ewbank opted to reward his son-in-law, Charley Winner, as his replacement.

And although he admittedly had a kickass name for a football coach, Winner was *not* a winner – going 9-14 in a little over a season and a half, before being fired three days after a 52-19 shellacking at the hands of the Colts in Week 9 of the 1975 season. Meanwhile, Michaels understandably did not appreciate being skipped over, and bolted to serve as the DC for the Philadelphia Eagles for three seasons.

However, he would return to the Jets as their DC in '76, and then finally be named HC in '77 – and became largely responsible for helping turn the franchise around by the early '80s/Sack Exchange era. And he possibly could have helped get things back on track a lot sooner (and the '70s may not have been a total washout for the franchise) if he was hired back in '72…instead of Winner.

68

Gastineau's Sack Dance Spawns Excessive Celebrations

Don't particularly care for players dancing and prancing after a big play – even if they are on an awful team that hasn't won a single stinking game until late in the season (*cough*, 2020 Jets, *cough*)? Well, we can all thank Mark Gastineau for trailblazing the art of "overzealous celebration." Granted, his brand of merriment was quite tame compared to what would come after, but still, at the time, it wasn't common for a player to celebrate in an overly animated fashion until the Jets' defensive end created his signature "Sack Dance." Although, Gastineau never really "danced" exactly the same way each time (after taking down an opposing team's QB) – it usually consisted of the Jets' defensive end flailing his arms.

And while the Sack Dance was usually harmless fun (although not very sportsmanlike towards your opponent), it did on at least one occasion lead to a bruhaha – on September 25, 1983, when Rams right tackle Jackie Slater took exception and shoved #99 from behind after he had sacked QB Vince Ferragamo and began dancing.

Immediately thereafter, countless members from both teams started punching and wrestling each other on the field (wearing helmets and pads prevented any injuries, thankfully) – resulting in a total of 37 players from both teams being fined. Regardless, we can all thank Mr. Gastineau for what eventually morphed into Odell Beckham impersonating a dog urinating, Isaiah Crowell mimicking wiping his derrière with a football, and Joe Horn pulling a cell phone out of a goalpost and making a call.

67

The Human Wall

Nobody likes a cheater. But only the Jets could cheat so obviously in a game…and *still* lose. On December 12, 2010 (week 14), the Jets were in a close (yet admittedly, ugly) game against the Dolphins at home, coming off a blowout 45-3 loss the week before versus (who else?) the Pats. With 3:11 left in the 3rd quarter, the Dolphins punted from their 14-yard line. When the play was over (Jets returner Santonio Holmes caught the ball and stepped out of bounds at about the Dolphins' 34-yard line), Miami cornerback Nolan Carroll was injured on the play – laying in pain on the white stripe just in front of the Jets sideline.

Replays showed that Carroll was the victim of a Human Wall.

And just what is a "Human Wall," you ask? Is it the name of a can't-miss formation or play? No. It's when several gentlemen not playing in the game – but who are employed by the Jets and wearing identical green warm-up suits – stand as close as possible to where the white line of the out of bounds marker meets the sideline (and standing next to each other, side-by-side), to deter a player from the other team to run too close. And replays showed that the first one in line in the Human Wall actually stuck his left knee out – which resulted in Carroll being tripped/hurt (at about the Jets' 33-yard line).

Soon after, it was determined that the "tripper" was Jets strength coach Sal Alosi (a position he had held since 2007, having previously been employed by the team as an assistant strength coach from 2002-2005). The day after the incident – oh by the way, the Jets lost the game, 10-6 – it was announced that Alosi was suspended without pay for the rest of the season and fined an additional $25,000 by the Jets for his role in the incident.

Then on December 30th, ESPN reported that the NFL had fined the Jets $100,000 "in the wake of discoveries involving strength and conditioning coach Sal Alosi, who instructed inactive players to stand in a wall in a prohibited area on the sideline to deter opposing teams' players during special-teams plays."

Alosi would resign from the Jets on January 31, 2011 (a little over a week after the Jets lost the AFC Championship Game to the Steelers), but would later find employment with the UCLA Bruins and working with Knicks point guard Derrick Rose.

Final score: Dolphins 10, Jets 6.

66

Beating This Winless Team Should Be a Breeze

"On any given Sunday, any team can beat any other team" is a famous saying pertaining to football. But when you lose to a team that went on to win only a single stinking game the entire year – and *you* represented the "1" in the win column – it stings just a little bit more. And it turns out that twice in the history of the Jets, they provided the lone win for teams that finished with a 1-15 record.

In 1980, they lost in week 15 to the Saints by a score of 21-20 (at Shea Stadium), and then fast-forward to 1991, they lost in week 11 to the Colts by a score of 28-27 (at Giants Stadium). And while it's a little easier to understand the 1980 Jets blunder since they finished a dismal 4-12, it's harder to make sense of the 1991 Jets, since they actually made the playoffs that year (although admittedly, with a .500 record).

Also worth mentioning, it looked as if the Jets could possibly add an additional third entry into this unwanted category in 2019, when the then-winless Dolphins – who looked like a team that was getting ready to tank (and had the 31st-ranked offense and 30th-ranked defense in the entire NFL) – were finally victorious in week 9 against none other than the J-E-T-S, Jets, Jets, Jets, and would use their surprise victory as a launching pad for their season, finishing 5-11 (including a surprising final game victory vs. the still-Brady-led Pats).

65

Matt Robinson's Sore Thumb

It is convenient to simply say that Richard Todd inherited the Jets QB job from Joe Namath – after Broadway Joe left for the west coast after the 1976 season. But long-time Jets fans can confirm, this was not the case. For a spell during the late '70s, the QB position was being battled out between Todd and a largely-forgotten gentleman, Matt Robinson. After taking over for an injured Todd during the 1978 season in week 5 (with the team stuck at 2 wins and 2 losses), Robinson led the Jets to an 8-8 record, and passed for over 2,000 yards in the process – a big improvement over the previous season's foul 3-11 mark. As a result, Robinson was named the starting QB for the 1979 season.

But then, the "Same Old Jets" curse reared its ugly head – Robinson endured a mysterious thumb injury (alleged to have been the result of horsing around off the field), which he did not reveal to the team right away. The Jets lost a tight one against the Cleveland Browns in the opening game of the '79 season in overtime, 25-22 (the story goes that they unwrapped Robinson's injured digit late in the game when it was assumed the Jets would be victorious, which led to the QB having problems gripping the ball when their assumptions were incorrect concerning the game's finality), and Coach Michaels was livid that the injury was not reported until it was too late – supposedly at the final practice the day before.

Due to the supposed cover-up, Todd reclaimed the QB starting spot from the next game onward, and another so-so 8-8 mark occurred. After the season, Robinson would be traded to the Broncos, and after '82, would be out of the NFL altogether. How talented and promising was Robinson at full health? To quote Jets cornerback Bobby Jackson in the book, *Sack Exchange*, "If he would have been our starting QB, I would be wearing a Super Bowl ring," and went on to call Robinson "A great leader who could throw on the run."

By this point, you probably know what time it is…time to add another entry into the dreaded "What if?" category.

64

Giving the Sanchize
an Extension

After two erratic but all-in-all successful seasons with the Jets in 2009 and 2010 (which saw the team make it to back-to-back AFC Championship Game appearances), hopes were high that Mark Sanchez would turn the corner and put together his first truly complete season from a consistency standpoint in 2011.

We were sadly mistaken.

Sanchez was again inconsistent, and the Jets floundered to an 8-8 mark and missed the playoffs. With it being made public that the Colts and Peyton Manning were parting ways in 2012 (since the Colts held the top pick in the draft, and were going to select Andrew Luck), there was a momentary buzz concerning Manning possibly landing with the Jets. But this was ultimately mere malarky, as #18 would sign on the dotted line with the Broncos.

But perhaps sensing that they may have hurt Sanchez's feelings concerning all the hubbub in the press about Manning potentially being a Jet (which if it did come to pass, they obviously would have severed ties with Sanchez), the Jets did an about face, and Sanchez signed a three-year extension with Gang Green (which included $20 million in guarantees).

Did this kind gesture on the Jets' part lead to Sanchez finally fulfilling his early promise? I'll use two words to answer that question – *Butt Fumble* (which occurred the following season).

After 2013, Sanchez would spread his wings and soar from the Jets to the Eagles, and be out of the NFL after 2018.

63

Re-signing Fitz

After Ryan Fitzpatrick led the Jets to a respectable 10-6 mark and a near-playoff berth in 2015 – plus putting up such stellar stats as 3,905 passing yards and 31 passing touchdowns (shattering Vinny Testaverde's 1998 franchise record for most touchdown passes in a season) against 15 interceptions – the Jets opted to re-sign the usually-bearded QB to a one-year, fully guaranteed $12 million contract.

Bad move.

Admittedly, after coming off such a strong season, only Nostradamus would have known that Fitzpatrick would stink up the joint in 2016 (over a thousand less passing yards, and 12 touchdowns against 17 interceptions). And in typical Same Old Jets style, after being benched in favor of both Geno Smith and Bryce Petty at various points in the season (yep, he was *that* bad), Fitzpatrick wound up starting the season's final game and led the Jets to a convincing win against the Buffalo Bills, 31-10.

What's so "SOJ" about that, you ask? These are the same Bills who the Fitz-led Jets could *not* beat when a playoff berth was there's for the taking, almost exactly one year earlier.

62

The Erosion of Revis Island

Since I began watching the NFL in the early '80s, there were few cornerbacks I've witnessed as dominating as Darrelle Revis in his prime. In fact, he became *so* dominating that a fitting nickname was bestowed upon him, "Revis Island," as a nod to his place in the secondary where he worked his magic on opposing receivers.

Who can forget how in just his second season (2008) he limited Randy Moss to a mere pair of catches and a measly 22 yards in a game against the Pats, not allowing Chad Ochocinco to catch a single bloody pass in the 2009 regular season finale (and limiting him to just two receptions for 28 yards the following week in the playoffs), or in the 2010 AFC Wildcard vs. the Colts, when he only allowed Reggie Wayne a single catch for one yard.

However, going into the 2012 season, there were some problems behind the scenes between Revis and Jets management concerning his contract not being reworked to his satisfaction. And after just the second game of the season, he was gone for the year – thanks to a torn ACL. In April 2013, Revis was traded to Tampa where he enjoyed a solid season, before signing on with the Pats for the 2014 campaign – during which he won a Super Bowl. When the Pats opted not to pick up an option to bring Revis back for a second year, the Jets welcomed him for an encore in 2015 – a five-year, $70 million contract with $39 million guaranteed.

I guess the Pats knew something that the Jets didn't, because Revis was a shell of his former self as a player – glaringly no longer the shut-down corner he once was. In fact, he was *so bad* during his second go-round with Gang Green that he was released by the team in early 2017, before landing with the Chiefs, and then, announcing his retirement a year later.

While it's tempting to think that the title of the Steve Miller classic, "Take the Money and Run," may sum up the last few years of Revis' career, it seemed like it was just a case of a player getting older and running out of gas. Which of course, the rest of the NFL could seemingly sense coming…but *not* the Jets.

61

Signing a Bad Newz QB

If you're trying to appease a fanbase that has been tormented for decades...perhaps employing a quarterback who was freed from prison a few years back for his role in a gruesome dogfighting ring is *not* a good idea. To back up a bit, there's no denying that for a spell, Michael Vick was one of the most dynamic and exciting players in the NFL. From 2001-2006 as a member of the Atlanta Falcons, Vick used his arm *and* legs to create game-changing plays.

But in August of 2007, that all came to an abrupt halt, when he pleaded guilty to federal charges of being involved in a dog fighting ring, Bad Newz Kennels, which operated on property owned by Vick in Surry County, Virginia – and being sentenced to 23 months in prison (but serving 18 months in federal prison and two months in home confinement). This resulted in Vick not playing football at all during the 2007 and 2008 seasons, before signing with the Eagles in 2009, and playing five seasons in the City of Brotherly Love.

Then, when Jets GM John Idzik opted to release Mark Sanchez in 2014, he decided to sign Vick to a one-year, $5 million contract. That season, he and Geno Smith served as a QB duo...and the Jets finished 4-12 – with Vick playing in ten games, starting three, and putting up the worst stats of his career up until that point. Mercifully, Vick was one-and-done with the Jets (signing with the Steelers for 2015, before retiring).

60

Gee, Broadway Joe Is Getting Injured a Lot These Days. Shouldn't We Find a Serviceable Back-up QB? *Nah.*

Between 1970-1976, Joe Namath played in more than 10 regular season games 4 times (all 14 in 1974 and '75, 13 in '72, and 11 in '76), and unquestionably, him missing significant playing time due to injuries in '70 (playing in only 5 games), '71 (4 games), and '73 (6 games) derailed those respective Jets seasons. It's somewhat forgivable for a team to get caught unprepared for a single season with an inadequate back-up quarterback when your starter goes down for a lengthy duration. But *several* seasons?

From 1969-1974, one of Broadway Joe's back-ups was a chap by the name of Al Woodall, who saw substantial playing time in '71 and '73, where the team went 1-4 and 1-5 during the stretches of games he started. Other best-forgotten back-up QB's employed by the Jets during this span included Bob Davis (1970-'72), Bill Demory (1973-'74), JJ Jones (1975), Steve Joachim (1976), and Richard Todd (1976, but this was a different situation, as the then-rookie was being groomed to be Namath's successor).

So the question remains…was Jets management truly that clueless that they wouldn't have tried to acquire better back-up QB's during this stretch, that were more talented, competitive, or just plain serviceable? And before younger readers of this book start to wonder, "Maybe all the other NFL teams committed the same faux pas?" – *hogwash*. Case in point, during the same era, the Raiders won with both Daryle Lamonica and Ken Stabler, the Colts with Johnny Unitas and Earl Morrall, the Cowboys with Roger Staubach and Craig Morton, etc.

Perhaps it's best to just leave this mystery unsolved.

59

The Last Jets Game at Shea

Usually, a pro sports team's last game at a stadium they have long called home is done so in style – thanking fans for their years of support with a pre or post-game ceremony, and even bringing back some of their all-time great players to wave to the crowd.

Not so if you were the Jets on the afternoon of December 10, 1983.

During the '83 season, it became known that the Jets were going to soar across the Hudson to co-inhabit Giants Stadium (fully explained why/how in entry #14). Yep, *only the Jets* – leaving one "shared stadium" for yet another "shared stadium."

So, on the 10th, the Jets hosted the Steelers. While the Jets' season had been disappointing, they were coming off a three-game winning streak, and at 7-7, were still in the playoff hunt. But instead of continuing their winning ways, the Jets got blown out (the last game that Hall of Famer Terry Bradshaw would ever play in) and denied the playoffs/ultimately finishing at an unsatisfactory 7-9.

After the game, displeased fans stormed the field, getting into confrontations with police, tearing down the two goal posts (I guess some of the more inebriated fans thought they could fit them in their car to take home?), and ripping up wooden bleachers.

Sayonara, Shea.

Final score: Steelers 34, Jets 7.

58

Goodbye Chad, Hello Brett

Although there's no denying that Chad Pennington was a great leader and solid QB during his career with the Jets, his inability to stay healthy and stay put on the football field was infuriating (and detrimental to the team). Sensing this (and understandably *fed up*), when the Jets had the opportunity to acquire future Hall of Famer Brett Favre from the Packers via trade (the asking price was a mere "conditional fourth-round pick in the 2009 NFL Draft with performance escalation") during the summer of 2008, it was an offer they couldn't refuse. So, in came Brett, and out went Chad (Pennington was immediately cut by the Jets, and wound up signing on with their division rivals, the Dolphins).

And for the first three-quarters of the 2008 season, it seemed like it was undoubtedly the right move for Gang Green – who were sitting pretty with an 8-3 record (including a thrilling OT win versus archrivals the Pats in week 11, 34-31), and with Favre seeming to have quickly found his groove with his new team. And the week after the victory over the Pats, Brett and the Jets manhandled the previously unbeaten Titans, 34-13 – leading many to dream of this being "the Jets' year."

Not so fast, buster.

It would later be revealed that during the Titans game, Brett injured his arm (a torn biceps tendon in his throwing shoulder), and rather than the Jets reporting the injury, they kept it hush-hush – which they would later be fined a cool $125k for. And it would also explain why Brett and the Jets played so awful over the final five games of the season, going 1-4, and missing the playoffs entirely (resulting in the firing of HC Eric Mangini a day after the season ended).

Chad? Oh, he just led the Dolphins to a surprising 11-5 record (including beating the Jets in the final game of the season in NJ, 24-17, squashing any remaining playoff fantasies that Gang Green had), a first place finish in the AFC East, a passer rating of 97.4, becoming the first Dolphins QB since Dan Marino to throw for 3,500 yards, and winning his second "Comeback Player of the Year" award.

Brett? He'd pull a "Brett Favre" – feigning retirement in order to leave the Jets, then signing on with the Vikings in time for the 2009 season (in which he *did* lead the team to the NFC Championship Game…but lost, 31-28, to the Saints in OT). Years later, we would also learn about Brett's alleged un-gentlemanly behavior towards several female Jets employees (more on that in the next two entries) during his lone year in NJ.

Guess the Jets would have been better off just sticking with ol' Chad, eh?

57

Sexual Harassment
in the Workplace (Part I)

If you're trying to win a woman's heart, perhaps consider sending flowers, chocolates, or some other appropriate gift...*not* creepy voicemail messages or alleged photographs of your fully exposed penis. But this was what briefly-tenured Jets QB Brett Favre was accused/suspected of in his lone season with the club (2008) – involving Jets "game day host," Jenn Sterger.

The story goes that Sterger (who has been photographed for such publications as *Maxim* and *Playboy*) caught the attention of Favre, which led to several voicemail messages from Favre to Sterger, requesting that they meet up – which then led to Sterger receiving the aforementioned photos (via text) of a certain part of the male anatomy. It's also worth pointing out that Favre was a married man (to Deanna Favre, since 1996).

Later, Favre admitted to leaving the voicemails to Sterger, but denied sending the photos (the NFL later disclosed, "Forensic analysis failed to establish that Favre sent the objectionable photographs to Sterger") – although a wristwatch can be seen in these photos that closely resembles a wristwatch that Favre wore at his press conference concerning his retirement from the Packers (on March 4, 2008).

Anyway, at some point the unsolicited correspondence stopped, and Favre eventually announced to the Jets he planned to retire on

February 11, 2009, and Sterger left her job with the team on May 7, 2009. But then in 2010, this all became public knowledge when Deadspin broke the story in August (with the audio of the voicemail messages surfacing shortly thereafter).

Favre would eventually be fined $50,000 (which was equivalent to only about five minutes of playing time, as his base salary that season was $11.6 million) by the NFL for what commissioner Roger Goodell called "Failure to cooperate with the investigation in a forthcoming manner," but was not suspended for a single game (Favre was a member of the Vikings by this point). Sterger would later be interviewed by such outlets as *Good Morning America* and *Nightline* about what happened – in which she explained how the scandal turned her life "upside down," and how it affected her family.

In an interview with Craig Carton and Evan Roberts on WFAN's *Carton & Roberts* in January 2021 (after briefly-tenured Mets GM Jared Porter was in the news after admitting to sending a photo of his exposed penis to a female reporter in 2016, resulting in his firing), Sterger – who now goes by the name Jennifer Decker, after marrying former MLB player Cody Decker – further discussed how the scandal affected both her professional and personal life.

And one of the more surprising things discussed during the appearance was that she had never even met Favre, which makes what he did even more incomprehensible and disturbing (of course, not that a meeting would have made this type of conduct acceptable).

Would Mr. Favre appreciate someone treating one of his daughters this way? I think not.

56

Sexual Harassment in the Workplace (Part II)

As if leaving inappropriate voicemail messages for Jenn Sterger wasn't bad enough, it came to light in 2011 that two former massage therapists for the Jets, Christina Scavo and Shannon O'Toole, had filed a lawsuit against the team, Brett Favre, and a team employee (Lisa Ripi) who supervised both women – for a similar reason.

The two women claimed that they had been fired by the team after Scavo's husband confronted Favre after his wife told him she was allegedly receiving – surprise, surprise – sexually suggestive texts from the eventual Hall of Fame QB in 2008 (O'Toole asserted she was fired because Scavo got her the job with Jets).

In 2013, a lawyer for both Scavo and O'Toole confirmed to *The Associated Press* that the case had been "resolved and discontinued" – but would not comment on what the terms of the settlement were.

55

Sexual Harassment in the Workplace (Part III)

The day after the Jets' 2010 season opener/cliff-hanger 10-9 loss to the Ravens on *Monday Night Football*, it was not just the specifics of the game that were being discussed in the press, but also, the team's treatment – or perhaps more fittingly, *mistreatment* – of a female reporter on assignment to interview Mark Sanchez a few days earlier (on Saturday, September 11th, at the team's practice facility in Florham Park, New Jersey).

Supposedly, several unnamed Jets players in the locker room catcalled a reporter for Mexico's TV Azteca television network, Inés Sainz, while it was also reported in *The Associated Press* that "During defensive drills on Saturday, Jets assistant coach Dennis Thurman seemed to deliberately throw to players near where Sainz was standing on the sideline. Even linebacker Jason Taylor, who normally doesn't participate in those position drills, went out for a pass."

An article penned three years later for ESPN by Jane McManus said that not only did other reporters on the scene feel uncomfortable about what was going on around them, but that Jets nose tackle Kris Jenkins went as far as declaring (or in McManus' description, *roaring*) "This is our locker room!" Sainz would later go on to tweet that she was "dying of embarrassment" and that the atmosphere in the locker room was "uncomfortable."

Additionally, Sainz was quoted in the aforementioned *Associated Press* article as saying, "Of course you feel it when you are being stared at and when you are being spoken of in a certain way. I opted to ignore it...I tried to not even pay attention."

To the credit of Jets owner Woody Johnson, when he found out about what had taken place, he personally apologized to Sainz, and in the same aforementioned ESPN article, it was reported that he had "volunteered to fund a league-wide program to educate NFL players and teams about sexual harassment."

Meanwhile, Washington Redskins running back Clinton Portis called into a Washington, D.C. radio show to discuss the topic of women reporters in men's locker rooms shortly after the Sainz incident, and was quoted as saying, "You sit in the locker room with 53 guys, and all of the sudden you see a nice woman in the locker room, I think men are gonna tend to turn and look and want to say something to that woman" (a statement that Portis later apologized for).

To borrow a point made from the earlier "Sexual Harassment in the Workplace (Part I)" entry, would Mr. Portis or the rowdy Jets players/personnel have had the same views or behaved in the same manner towards Sainz if this happened to be their daughter, wife, mother, etc.?

54

Gregg Williams' Incomprehensible Play Call

Your team is sitting on an 0-11 record and is the laughingstock of the league. You are on the verge of finally winning your first game of the year – with your team ahead 28-24, with mere seconds left to play. But instead of putting some effort into actually calling a defensive scheme that could possibly *win* the game…let's offer up an atrocious play call to easily set up the opposing team to score a touchdown and win! That's certainly what it seems Jets DC Gregg Williams pulled in a contest on December 6, 2020, against the Raiders at MetLife Stadium.

The Raiders got the ball back at their 39-yard line with 35 seconds left to go in the game and no time outs, and then found themselves at the Jets' 46-yard line with only 13 seconds left on the board. That was when Gregg Williams sealed his fate with an unwise call – a "Cover 0" play.

For those not fluent in football jargon, it basically means that there is no safety behind to lend a hand in coverage – as the Jets opted to have seven players blitz Raiders QB Derek Carr. Jets safety Matthias Farley was just behind the seven rushing Jets, as to cover Carr in case he decided to run for it (if you were wondering about the remaining three Jets defensemen, they were playing man coverage against three Raider receivers).

But there was a rather unfair advantage – WR Henry Ruggs against rookie CB Lamar Jackson. And before you knew it, Jackson was a few steps behind Ruggs, Carr lobbed the ball easily to Ruggs, and the Raiders were now ahead by three points. And with only five seconds left in the game, the Raiders easily held on for the victory.

The immediate result? Williams was handed his walking papers the very next day by the Jets. But it turns out that Williams was not entirely to blame – Jets HC Adam Gase admitted after the game that he regretted not calling a timeout to switch the play before it happened. In other words, Gase *knew* about this senseless play call…and allowed it to happen, anyway.

Don't feel bad, Gregg. Adam would also be gone soon – less than a month later.

Final Score: Raiders 31, Jets 28.

53

"I'm seeing ghosts"

Ghosts can be of the welcomed variety (*Caspar the Friendly Ghost*) or the unwelcomed variety (*Poltergeist*). And if you were Sam Darnold during a nightmarish 33-0 loss against the Patriots in week 7 of the 2019 season, they would fall under the latter category. Wearing a mic during the game, Darnold was heard saying the now-classic phrase, "I'm seeing ghosts," after being whacked around mercilessly by the Pats' D (with the Jets already down 24-0 at that point).

After offering up such putrid game stats as 11 of 32 for a measly 86 yards, 4 interceptions, 1 fumble, and 0 TD's, *I'd* admit to seeing ghosts, too. While speaking to the press shortly after uttering that paranormally-tinged phrase, he explained its meaning – "I've just got to see the field a lot better, that's kinda what that means."

And in case you were wondering, no, the "I'm seeing ghosts game" did *not* occur on Halloween (but close, just about a week away – October 21st).

52

"I want to kiss you"

There was obviously a reason why Joe Namath earned the nickname "Broadway Joe" – as he seemed to enjoy the extracurricular activities that fame can bring you as a sports superstar playing for a New York team, especially during the wild n' crazy '60s and '70s. In fact, two specific quotes from the man himself provided clues to his main interests at the time – "It seems almost un-American to me for a bachelor not to go around and have a drink with a lady now and then" and "I like my Johnny Walker Red and my women blonde."

But by the early 21st century, Namath's alcoholism had gotten the best of him – he allegedly blamed it for the break-up of his marriage to his wife Deborah Mays, and it was embarrassingly on display for all to see on the evening of December 20, 2003, during a live TV interview with ESPN's Suzy Kolber.

While the Jets were playing a game against the Patriots (why oh why do the Pats seem to often be involved in Gang Green's most uncomfortable moments?), Kolber asked the question, "What does it mean to you now when the team is struggling?" An obviously inebriated Namath leaned close to the reporter for a second, before awkwardly replying, "I want to kiss you" (and even repeating the phrase again later in the interview).

However, this negative event did lead to a positive in Namath's life – in his 2020 book, *All the Way: My Life in Four Quarters*, he said that it led to him stopping drinking alcohol entirely.

51

Broadway Joe "Retires"

Somewhat forgotten in Joe Namath's colorful career was that while still basking in the glow of the Jets' improbable Super Bowl III victory, he retired entirely from football. Admittedly, it was short-lived, but still, the thought of the team without their charismatic leader caused agita amongst Jets fans (and most certainly, with the team's management).

The story goes that Namath along with two other gents – singer/actor Bobby Van and former Jets safety Ray Abruzzese – opened up a bar/nightclub in the spring of '69, located at 798 Lexington Avenue in New York City. Entitled "Bachelors III" (since all three of its owners were bachelors), the establishment proved to be popular...but maybe a little *too* popular for NFL commissioner Pete Rozelle's liking – allegedly, members of organized crime were part of its clientele.

As a result, Rozelle gave Namath a choice – either give up his interest in Bachelors III or be suspended. Instead of selling, Namath chose retirement (which he announced in an emotional press conference, in which he shed a tear). Soon realizing that he was throwing away a golden opportunity with the Jets, Namath changed his mind and was back with the team in time for training camp – although with the stipulation that Namath sell his portion of Bachelors III (which he agreed to do).

50

The Fireman "Retires"

What does it take for a "super fan" to turn their back on their beloved team? The Jets' longtime "J-E-T-S" chant leader, Fireman Ed (real name: Edwin M. Anzalone), answered this question after an unpleasant occurrence on Thanksgiving evening, 2012 – during a blowout loss against the Patriots on national television, 49-19 (which birthed one of the biggest Jets blunders in their entire history…more on that later). Anzalone would later explain to NBC New York that at halftime of this dud of a game, he was supposedly accosted by two mean men in a restroom at MetLife Stadium.

That was the breaking point (he also claimed in the same article that he had received substantial harassment in the stands over the years – including being verbally abused, spat on, and beer spilt upon). So, on November 25, 2012, the man known for wearing a white fireman's hat (with a Jets logo) and sporting either a Bruce Harper or Mark Sanchez jersey announced that he was to no longer attend Jets games and lead the famous chant. The retirement didn't last forever though – Anzalone did return in the season-opener vs. the Browns on September 13, 2015 (a 31-10 Jets victory), and since the start of the 2019 season, had seemingly returned to attending games.

49

Goodbye USA, Hello UK

After Woody Johnson became the Jets' owner in 2000, the team has seen its share of ups (two back-to-back AFC Championship appearances, Darrelle Revis in his prime, etc.) and downs (late season choke-jobs, multiple losing seasons, etc.). And the same year that the 45th President of the United States, Donald Trump, was sworn into office, an interesting bit of news surfaced for fans of Gang Green – Woody would be serving as the "United States Ambassador to the United Kingdom."

As a result, Woody would hand the reins of his football team to his brother, Christopher Johnson, so he could focus solely on his new position overseas. Woody's tenure as USAttUK would last from November 8, 2017 to January 20, 2021, and during that time when Christopher was in charge of the team, the Jets went 5-11 (2017), 4-12 (2018), 7-9 (2019), and 2-14 (2020), for a combined record of 18-46 (not to mention such disasters as the hiring of Adam Gase, the signing/mishandling of Le'Veon Bell, and the trading of Jamal Adams).

Yuck.

48

Jawbreaker

"Protect the quarterback" is one of the most important things stressed in football. But I guess one-time Jets' defensive end IK Enemkpali (full name: Ikemefuna Chinedum Enemkpali) thought that only pertained to players on the offensive line. In a true "only the Jets" moment, during the 2015 preseason (August 11th to be exact), Enemkpali sucker punched Jets QB Geno Smith in the face – later learned it was over a squabble concerning a measly $600 that Smith supposedly owed Enemkpali.

The aftermath? Smith suffered a broken jaw (and lost his QB job to Ryan Fitzpatrick) and Enemkpali was cut from the team. But this preposterous story doesn't just end there. The man who the Jets had just fired as their HC a few months prior, Rex Ryan, was now the HC of the Buffalo Bills…and he promptly hired Enemkpali for *his* team! And yes, it was *that* Bills squad that beat the Jets the last game of the season (see entry #41) – preventing a Jets playoff berth (despite finishing the season with a respectable 10-6 mark).

47

Putting Sanchez in a Meaningless Pre-Season Game

Picture this – it's the second to last game of the Jets' 2013 preseason, and they're a team that seems to not be 100% sure as to which of two quarterbacks (Mark Sanchez or rookie Geno Smith) they should commit to for the ensuing regular season. So, what did Jets HC Rex Ryan do? He decided to insert one of the two competing QB's in a meaningless game against the Giants in the middle of the 4th quarter, behind an offensive line comprised of a bunch of no-name/inexperienced players.

The result? You guessed it – a shoulder injury to Sanchez (after being manhandled by defensive tackle Marvin Austin) that required season-ending shoulder surgery, and the starting job being awarded to Smith…who clearly wasn't up to the task, as the Jets skidded to an 8-8 record that season. Also of note – that Jets-Giants preseason contest would be the last game Sanchez would play as a Jet, as he would be a Philadelphia Eagle the following season.

46

Not Going to Ray Lucas Sooner in 1999

When Vinny Testaverde went down in the opening game of the 1999 season (a season that many picked the Jets to build upon their previous season's success), coach Bill Parcells made the head-scratching decision to go with punter Tom Tupa as Testaverde's initial replacement, before handing the reins over to back-up QB Rick Mirer in the 4th quarter. And as we soon found out, the Mirer experiment was a bomb – as the Jets skidded to a 2-6 start.

Then, Parcells opted to promote a gentleman who was used primarily for surprise plays, Ray Lucas. And wouldn't ya know it, the team rallied around Lucas – who turned out to be the "anti-Mirer" – going 6-2. Only one itty bitty problem…the change was made too late. Finishing at 8-8, the Jets narrowly missed the playoffs. And by the time the 2000 season rolled around, Vinny's Achilles was fully healed, and he got the damn ball – with Lucas back to being a back-up, before playing for the Dolphins for two seasons, and then winding down his career with the Ravens in 2003.

I'm afraid yet another "What if?", fellow Jets fans.

45

No More Giving Him
the Damn Ball

By 2000, probably the biggest star – and certainly, the most out-spoken – player on the Jets was WR Keyshawn Johnson. After all, he had no problem speaking his mind (calling teammates Wayne Chrebet a "team mascot" and Neil O'Donnell "a stiff puppet" in his 1997 book, *Just Give Me the Damn Ball!*).

But he could also back up all the talk on the field – look no further than his "one man show" performance in the 1999 AFC Divisional Round Game vs. the Jaguars (in which he accumulated 121 yards and a touchdown via catching 9 passes, an additional 28 yards and another touchdown via rushing, recovering a fumble, *and* intercepting a pass on defense – resulting in a 34-24 victory and a trip to the AFC Championship Game).

But after the Jets' disappointing season the following year (missing the playoffs) and a rapid three-way hand-off of head coaches (Parcells > Belichick > Groh), friction was growing between Johnson and the Jets. Supposedly, the then-2x Pro Bowler wanted the last two years of his contract reworked – which the Jets declined to do – which led to some press bickering between Johnson and just-appointed HC Groh.

Ultimately, Groh won the battle – Johnson would be traded to the Buccaneers on April 12, 2000 for a pair of first round draft choices (which resulted in the Jets selecting DE John Abraham at #13 and TE Anthony Becht at #27, overall).

And while Johnson enjoyed success in Florida (including the Bucs defeating the Raiders in Super Bowl XXXVII), you could make the argument that he may have been better off remaining in the spotlight of the Big Apple, as he only lasted three-and-a-half seasons with the Bucs before another falling out occurred, and retiring after the 2006 season with good – but not quite "Hall of Fame worthy" – numbers.

Still, the prospect of an at-full-health Chad Pennington regularly tossing the ball to Keyshawn could have possibly taken the Jets to the Promised Land...but we'll never know.

44

Firing Pete Carroll
After One Season

The Jets were mediocre at best during the early '90s (two losing records and two .500 records between 1990-1993, with Bruce Coslet at the helm), and their defensive coordinator during this time was a chap by the name of Pete Carroll. So it wasn't the most explosively exciting announcement when Carroll was handed the Jets' head coaching job for the 1994 season.

However, under Carroll's guidance, by week 13, the Jets had cruised to a pleasantly-surprising season – with a 6-5 record, they were facing their archrival, the Miami Dolphins, at home in a battle for first place. However – and admittedly, a *big* however – the Jets lost a game in a way that only the Jets can (see entry #5 for all the gruesome details). What happened next? The Jets dropped their next five games, to end the season with a lackluster 6-10 mark.

Instead of keeping in mind that the Jets were competitive for most of the season before their collapse, higher ups decided that Carroll would be one-and-done as the team's HC – instead, giving the keys to the kingdom to Mr. Richard Edward Kotite, which led to some of the darkest days of the Jets' entire existence (that is, until Adam Gase came along).

What did Carroll do post-Jets? He had a few more NFL jobs in the late '90s (49ers DC from 1995-96 and Patriots' HC from 1997-99), before jumping to college football – where he fared far better.

Serving as the HC of USC from 2001-09, the team enjoyed two BCS Championship Game appearances (including a win in 2005) and ESPN.com named USC the #1 team of the decade between 1996 and 2006.

And in 2010, Carroll returned to the NFL as the HC of the Seahawks – including a Super Bowl XLVIII win in 2014 (at the Jets' home, MetLife Stadium, of all places). But admittedly, he is also responsible for one of the worst play calls in NFL history which resulted in a heartbreaking Super Bowl XLIX loss to the Patriots the following year (and made cornerback Malcolm Butler an instant folk hero to Massachusetts-based sports fans).

But still, wouldn't it have been better if the Jets held on to Carroll a little bit longer than just 1994? Judging from the stench of the Jets' next few seasons – *no question.*

43

The Idzik 12

If you or I were to pick twelve players in an NFL draft, chances are, we would at least land *one* keeper. So that makes it all the more astonishing that the Jets' general manager, John Idzik Jr., whiffed on *all twelve* selections of the 2014 draft. In case you forgot who these best-forgotten selections were, they included:

1. Round 1, selection #18: **Calvin Pryor, S**
2. Round 2, selection #49: **Jace Amaro, TE**
3. Round 3: selection #80: **Dexter McDougle, CB**
4. Round 4: selection #104: **Jalen Saunders, WR**
5. Round 4: selection #115: **Shaq Evans, WR**
6. Round 4: selection #137: **Dakota Dozier, OL**
7. Round 5: selection #154: **Jeremiah George, LB**
8. Round 6: selection #195: **Brandon Dixon, CB**
9. Round 6: selection #209: **Quincy Enunwa, WR**
10. Round 6: selection #210: **IK Enemkpali, LB**
11. Round 6: selection #213: **Tajh Boyd, QB**
12. Round 7: selection #233: **Trevor Reilly, LB**

By the time of this book's release (seven years after the fact), not a single draft selection that comprised "The Idzik 12" was still playing for the Jets. Heck, most of them were not even playing professional football anymore. Well, Mr. Idzik at least had one thing going for him after the stench had dissipated from this doo-doo draft – he hadn't selected Johnny Manziel (who the Browns regretfully picked at #22).

But because of this dumpster fire of a Jets draft (and also failing to fill the team's roster holes with serviceable talent), fans were understandably irritated – the low point being on November 5, 2014, when a plane circled the team's practice field for roughly 20 minutes, displaying a banner which read, "FIRE JOHN IDZIK."

After two lackluster seasons of Idzik as GM (in which the Jets went 8-8 and 4-12), Jets fans finally got their wish on December 29, 2014.

42

All They Need to Do Is Beat the Lions to Get Into the Playoffs

Bill Parcells' first year with the Jets was a memorable one – as he miraculously turned around a team that went 1-15 the previous year (under the iconic Rich Kotite) into a playoff contender. In fact, after week 13, it seemed like a forgone conclusion that the Jets would be playoff-bound that year – sitting pretty with an 8-4 record. *Not so fast*. Back-to-back losses vs. the Bills (20-10) and the Colts (22-14) occurred, before the Jets blew out the Bucs, 31-0, which set up a season finale vs. the Lions in Detroit with the stakes set high – if the Jets win they're in, if they lose they're out.

Things certainly seemed promising for the Jets early on – as they jumped out to a 10-0 lead in the 1st quarter thanks to a John Hall FG and an Adrian Murrell rushing TD. And then…that was it for the Jets, as they endured several killer interceptions (including a Ray Lucas pass picked off in the end zone), while Hall of Fame RB Barry Sanders led the Lions – crossing 2,000 yards rushing for the season, in the process – to a slim margin of victory (although it did come with a steep price, when Detroit LB Reggie Brown suffered a spinal cord injury and never played another game).

Bye-bye playoffs.

Final score: Lions 13, Jets 10.

41

All They Need to Do Is Beat the Bills to Get Into the Playoffs

In Todd Bowles' first season as the Jets head coach, there were plenty of maddening twists and turns of inconsistency (something that seemed to plague the team throughout Bowles' 2015-2018 tenure as HC). But his first year was the most painful of the bunch, because they came *oh so close* to making the playoffs…and did not. And in true Jets fashion, they seemingly did all the heavy lifting in order to put themselves in an ideal position…but could not topple a feeble team in the final week to punch their playoff ticket.

Going into week 12, the Jets stood at .500. And throughout December, were the hottest team in the NFL, including impressive victories against the Giants in OT (23-20), and most memorably, against their archrivals the Patriots in OT (26-20), in the second to last game of the season. So, with the Jets facing the 7-8 Bills in Buffalo (with old pal Rex Ryan serving as Bills HC), obviously, Bowles' team would be well prepared and fired up for such a game, right?

Wrong.

QB Ryan Fitzpatrick (who along with wide receiver Brandon Marshall, was hoping to qualify for his first-ever NFL playoffs) had a simply *horrendous* game – including a whopping three interceptions…in the 4th quarter alone. And of course, they kept their fans on the edge of their seat and offered glimpses of hope, and in true Same Old Jets style, remained in the game until the final moments – blowing countless golden opportunities in the process.

As a great judge/golfer once said, "You'll get nothing and like it!"

Final score: Bills 22, Jets 17.

40

Ken, Al, and Freeman's
Playoff Swan Song

During the mid to late '80s, three of the top Jets offensive weapons were QB Ken O'Brien, RB Freeman McNeil, and WR Al Toon. But by the early '90s, the trio was rapidly reaching the end of their playing careers (with O'Brien exiting the Jets after 1992 and retiring after '93, and both McNeil and Toon retiring after '92). But all had one last playoff hurrah with Gang Green in 1991.

The '91 Jets remain one of the more befuddling teams of the franchise's history – coached by Bruce Coslet, the team wound up making the playoffs with a mere 8-8 record, whereas other more talented Jets teams with actual *winning* records (especially 2015's 10-6 team) failed to qualify for the playoffs.

But their so-so win-loss record made sense when you dug a bit deeper into their stats – finishing towards the middle-of-the-road in both offensive and defensive rankings (#11 and #10, respectively), not getting blown out by any of their opponents in their 8 losses (with the majority of their non-wins decided by either a touchdown or less, or a field goal or less), but one of those losses being an embarrassment concerning who they lost to (remember entry #66?).

And after they beat the Dolphins in the final game of the season in an overtime thriller (23-20), the Jets were paired with the Houston Oilers for the Wild Card round – on December 29th at the

Astrodome. Led by QB Warren Moon, the Oilers had quite a potent offense – featuring three exceptional wide receivers (Curtis Duncan, Drew Hill, and Ernest Givens).

By early in the 4th quarter, it was still anyone's game, as the Oilers led by only a single TD, 17-10. However, a few costly blunders (O'Brien getting intercepted in the red zone and McNeil being stuffed on 4th and inches in the red zone) proved to be the difference makers in the game's outcome.

Not to mention two instances where the refs proved to be both clueless *and* useless. First, not calling an obvious hold committed on Toon on 4th down with less than 3:30 remaining in the game. Second, not stopping the clock after Jets TE Mark Boyer caught a pass from O'Brien just inside Houston territory with only 41 seconds left, and then three Oilers purposely lay on top of him after the tackle, and made no effort to get up (despite the Jets having no time outs remaining, the refs reserve the right to stop the clock in such situations of poor sportsmanship) – which brought the game time down to a mere 20 seconds.

But the Jets still had two more shots at glory. Shot #1: Toon letting a Hail Mary pass slip right through his fingers at the 1-yard line. Shot #2: Oilers SS Bubba McDowell intercepting a second Hail Mary pass to end the game.

And with that, the Jets provided fans with their usually-annual dose of disappointment right around the dawn of the new year.

Final score: Oilers 17, Jets 10.

39

The Last Jets
Playoff Game at Shea

The Jets' 1981 regular season was full of highlights – including a 26-7 thumping of their cross-river rivals the Giants (at the Jets' soon-to-be home, Giants Stadium), a thrilling last-second 16-15 victory over the Dolphins, and probably most memorable of all, a final-game blowout victory at home against the Packers, 28-3, which clinched the Jets' first playoff appearance in over ten years with a 10-5-1 record.

And it turns out that the Wildcard Playoff Game would be held at Shea (on December 27th) against the Buffalo Bills – a team they had already beaten at home in week 7, 33-14. Surely, the momentum of going 7-1 during the final two months of the season and playing in front of a rabid home crowd would spur the Jets to a fast start, right?

No way.

Usually sure-handed Jets kick returner Bruce Harper fumbled the opening kickoff, which was returned by the Bills' Charles Romes for a touchdown. Before you knew it, the suddenly mistake-prone Jets were deep in a hole in the 2nd quarter, 24-0. But to the Jets' credit, they refused to die, and by halftime, had cut into the Bills' lead, 24-10.

And they kept battling in the second half – and wound up with the ball with 2:36 remaining on the clock and trailing the Bills by only 4 points. Jets QB Richard Todd led Gang Green all the way downfield to the Bills' 11-yard line – with the Shea crowd going bananas – before Bills defensive back Bill Simpson (no relation to OJ) intercepted Todd on the 1-yard line with two seconds left in the game, to preserve a Bills victory.

And provide the obligatory crushing Jets playoff loss.

Final score: Bills 31, Jets 27.

38

Should We Secure the #1 Pick? No. We Should Not.

The 2020 season was on track to go down as the Jets' worst ever. And that's certainly saying something, as the franchise has constructed quite a few humdingers of awful seasons over the years (take your pick of either of the two Kotite seasons, for starters). But there was something that just felt *special* about 2020 as the season dragged on – whether it was the atrocious play calling of Adam Gase and Gregg Williams, the sad regression of Sam Darnold, two of the team's top talents being jettisoned to other teams, etc.

And by week 15, the Jets sat at 0-13, with only 3 more games to go – before they would join the lowly likes of the 1960 Dallas Cowboys, the 1976 Tampa Bay Buccaneers, the 1982 Baltimore Colts, the 2008 Detroit Lions, and the 2017 Cleveland Browns as being one of the select few NFL teams to not win a single bloody game for an entire season.

Usually, if you're sitting un-pretty with an 0-13 record, you have already locked up the #1 pick. But come on…this is the Jets! There was actually *one other team* that was sitting right next to the Jets on the dung heap, the Jacksonville Jaguars – with a nearly as putrid 1-12 mark. And with the Jets' final games against two teams that were fighting for a playoff spot (the Rams and Browns) and a team that always appears to have their number (the Pats), it seemed quite feasible that they were swirling rapidly down the toilet to a 0-16 mark.

Then, a funny thing happened…the Jets suddenly awoke from their coma and reeled off a pair of back-to-back wins against the Rams (23-20) and the Browns (23-16), before expectedly, bowing to Belichick, 28-14. Finishing with one more win than the Jags, the Jets lost out on the #1 pick, and fell to #2 – to the dissatisfaction of many Jets fans and regional sports columnists/radio personalities.

But I will admit, I am in the apparent minority who wanted to see the Jets win at least a single game, because the albatross around the franchise's neck for all of eternity as being one of the few winless-for-an-entire-season NFL teams may have been too much to bear (in so much that you can go on to win multiple Super Bowls, but some wisenheimer would remind you, "Yeah…but the Jets also didn't win *a single stinking game* in 2020").

Mission accomplished. Bye-bye #1 pick (which turned out to be Trevor Lawrence, selected by the Jaguars).

37

The Final 5 of '86

To borrow a quote from my book, *Sack Exchange: The Definitive Oral History of the 1980s New York Jets*, when asked about the Jets' 1986 season, WR Wesley Walker replied "I remember us being 10-1. I thought at that point in time – and still do – barring injuries, that was the best team the Jets ever had during my era. I thought we were definitely going to the Super Bowl. Every phase of our game was really pretty good."

Unfortunately the football gods frowned upon the "barring injuries" part. Most of the team's top talent (Mark Gastineau, Joe Klecko, Marty Lyons, etc.) all suffered injuries around the same time, and as a result, the once super-promising Jets season became totally derailed – as they dropped the final 5 games of the regular season (3 of which were embarrassing ass-kickings, 45-3 against the Dolphins, 45-24 against the Steelers, and 52-21 against the Bengals).

Finishing with a record of 10-6, the Jets wound up in second place (a game behind AFC East champs the Patriots) and would limp into the playoffs. And how did they fare in their quest for Super Bowl XXI? You'll read all about it in entry #8.

36

Free Agent Failures

Seemingly, for every Jets free agent signing success story (Curtis Martin, Kevin Mawae, Bart Scott, Vinny Testaverde, Wayne Chrebet, etc.), there are multiple stinkers. In fact, there are probably *so many* bad free agent signings that the Jets have fallen victim to that we will only pick a few that truly stand out from the pack (in no particular order). So, here we go:

Le'Veon Bell (running back): Rushed for 1,268 yards (2016) and 1,291 yards (2017) while with the Steelers, before sitting out 2018, and signing with the Jets for 4 years, $52.5 million. In his lone full season with the Jets (2019) he rushed for only 789 yards, and then in two games the following season, a mere 74 yards – before being released and signing with the Chiefs.

Neil O'Donnell (quarterback): After leading the Steelers to Super Bowl XXX in 1996 (albeit a loss to the Cowboys), O'Donnell signed with the Jets the next season for 5 years, $25 million. However, he had the misfortune of playing for HC Rich Kotite in the last year of his miserable 2-year stint (which saw the Jets go 1-15), and was knocked out for the season with a shoulder injury after playing in six games. The following year, the QB butted heads with new HC Bill Parcells, which saw him lose the starting job to Glenn Foley, before demanding a trade in the off-season (he would land with the Bengals).

Sam Cowart (linebacker): A Pro Bowler with the Bills in 2000, Cowart signed with the Jets 2 years later for 6 years, $31 million, and over the next 3 seasons, started only 3 (!) games.

Derrick Mason (wide receiver): 2x Pro Bowler with the Ravens who signed with the Jets in 2011 for 2 years, $3.8 million, and played in only 5 games the first year (and compiling such "stellar" stats as 13 receptions for a grand total of 115 yards), before being traded to the Texans in October, and a year later, retiring altogether.

Damien Robinson (safety): Signed with the Jets in 2001 for 5 years, $10 million, was gone after 2 years. It's never a good thing when you're a football player best known for an infamous facemask grab against the Saints that led to an altercation with the hot-headed Kyle Turley (who then flung your helmet high in the air) or for being arrested on the day of a game when an assault rifle is found in the trunk of your car in the parking lot of Giants Stadium (which occurred on October 14, 2001 – barely a month after 9/11) than for your contributions on the gridiron.

Honorable mentions of once great players that signed on with the Jets at the twilight of their career and…well, I think you know the rest: **Ronnie Lott, Art Monk, Boomer Esiason, Ty Law, Ed Reed, Steve Atwater, Brett Favre, LaDainian Tomlinson, Darrelle Revis** (remember entry #62?), etc.

35

Dreadful Draft Whiffs

Some teams have made an art form out of smart drafting – building championships due to scouting players, studying college player film, and/or crafty maneuvering on draft day (for example, the Steel Curtain-era Steelers, the Pats once Bill B signed on, etc.).

The Jets are most certainly *not* one of those teams. True, the franchise has landed a few plumb draft picks throughout their history (Joe Namath, John Riggins, Darrelle Revis, etc.), but it seems like for every success story, there are multiple blunders. So now, how about some players the Jets failed to draft, who were still available when it was their turn in line (in chronological order)?

In 1965, the Jets selected **Tom Nowatzke** at #4 (who opted to sign with the Detroit Lions). **Gale Sayers** would be selected at #5 (by the Chiefs, but would sign with the Bears), **Dick Butkus** at #9 (by the Broncos, but would sign with the Bears), and **Fred Biletnikoff** at #11 (by the Raiders). Although let's give the Jets some credit…they *did* pick Joe Namath at #1.

In 1973, the Jets selected **Burgess Owens** at #13 and **Robert Woods** at #38. **Dan Fouts** would be selected at #64 (by the Chargers).

In 1974, the Jets selected **Carl Barzilauskas** at #6, **Gordon Browne** at #31, **Godwin Turk** at #58, and **Roscoe Word** at #74. **Lynn Swan** would be selected at #21 (by the Steelers), **Jack**

Lambert at #46 (by the Steelers), **John Stallworth** at #82 (by the Steelers), and **Mike Webster** at #125 (by the Steelers).

In 1978, the Jets selected **Chris Ward** at #4. **James Lofton** would be selected at #6 (by the Packers) and **Ozzie Newsome** at #23 (by the Browns).

In 1980, the Jets selected **Johnny "Lam" Jones** at #2. **Anthony Muñoz** would be selected at #3 (by the Bengals) and **Art Monk** at #18 (by the Redskins).

In 1983, the Jets selected **Ken O'Brien** at #24. **Dan Marino** would be selected at #27 (by the Dolphins).

In 1985, the Jets selected **Al Toon** at #10. **Jerry Rice** would be selected at #16 (by the 49ers).

In 1988, the Jets selected **Dave Cadigan** at #8 and **Terry Williams** at #37. **Michael Irvin** would be selected at #11 (by the Cowboys) and **Thurman Thomas** at #40 (by the Bills).

In 1990, the Jets selected **Blair Thomas** at #2. **Junior Seau** would be selected at #5 (by the Chargers) and **Emmitt Smith** at #17 (by the Cowboys).

In 1995, the Jets selected **Kyle Brady** at #9, **Hugh Douglas** at #16, and **Matt O'Dwyer** at #33. **Warren Sapp** would be selected at #12 (by the Buccaneers), **Ty Law** at #23 (by the Patriots), and **Curtis Martin** at #74 (by the Patriots).

In 2000, the Jets selected **Shaun Ellis** at #12, **John Abraham** at #13, **Chad Pennington** at #18, **Anthony Becht** at #27, **Laveranues Coles** at #78, **Windrell Hayes** at #143, and **Tony Scott** at #179. **Tom Brady** would be selected at #199 (by the Patriots).

In 2003, the Jets selected **Dewayne Robertson** at #4. **Troy Polamalu** would be selected at #16 (by the Steelers).

In 2012, the Jets selected **Quinton Coples** at #16. **Russell Wilson** would be selected at #75 (by the Seahawks).

In 2017, the Jets selected **Jamal Adams** at #6. **Patrick Mahomes** would be selected at #10 (by the Chiefs).

In 2018, the Jets selected **Sam Darnold** at #3. **Josh Allen** would be selected at #7 (by the Bills) and **Lamar Jackson** at #32 (by the Ravens).

34

Dreadful Draft Picks

We have already analyzed the worst draft "whiffs" by the Jets over the years. So now, how about ten of the worst draft picks (in no particular order)?

Vernon Gholston (defensive end): Selected in the first round (6th overall) of the 2008 draft. Signed a five-year deal worth $32 million ($21 million guaranteed). From 2008-2010 with the Jets, did not record a single sack, forced fumble, nor fumble recovery (out of the NFL after 2012).

Blair Thomas (running back): Selected in the first round (2nd overall) of the 1990 draft. From 1990-1993, rushed for 2,009 yards and 5 TD's (out of the NFL after 1995).

Dee Milliner (cornerback): Selected in the first round (9th overall) of the 2013 draft. Signed a fully guaranteed four-year deal worth $12.66 million (that included a $7.58 million signing bonus). From 2013-2016, was benched three times in his rookie season, played only three games in 2014 due to a torn Achilles tendon, and only five games in 2015 due to wrist surgery (out of the NFL after 2016).

Johnny "Lam" Jones (wide receiver): Selected in the first round (2nd overall) of the 1980 draft. From 1980-1984, caught 13 TD's, started in 36 games (out of the NFL after 1987).

Calvin Pryor (strong safety): Selected in the first round (18th overall) of the 2014 draft. From 2014-2016, had 3 interceptions, 1 forced fumble, 0 fumble recoveries (out of the NFL after 2017).

Quinton Coples (defensive end): Selected in the first round (16th overall) of the 2012 draft. Signed a four-year deal worth $8.8 million. From 2012-2015, had 16.5 sacks and 2 forced fumbles (out of the NFL after 2016).

Kyle Brady (tight end): Selected in the first round (9th overall) of the 1995 draft. From 1995-1998, caught 10 TD's, 93 receptions for 949 yards. Unlike the others in this list, Brady had a decent NFL career (playing for the Jaguars and Patriots from 1999-2007), but is best known for who the Jets opted NOT to select in in favor of him in '95 (Warren Sapp).

Dewayne Robertson (defensive tackle): Selected in the first round (4th overall) of the 2003 draft. From 2003-2007, had 14.5 sacks and 3 forced fumbles (out of the NFL after 2008).

Roger Vick (fullback): Selected in the first round (21st overall) of the 1987 draft. From 1987-1989, rushed for 1,231 yards and 10 TD's (out of the NFL after 1990).

Christian Hackenberg (quarterback): Selected in the second round (51st overall) of the 2016 draft. Hackenberg stands out from the pack *so* much, that he was deserving of his own special entry in this book…up next.

33

The Most Perplexing Jets QB of All-Time?

During the Jets' history, they have employed the services of a seemingly infinite amount of quarterbacks whose talent left much to be desired (at least at a pro level). But the one that just may stand alone at the peak of the Mt. Everest of dud Jets QB's is…Christian Hackenberg.

That said, Hackenberg *did* turn heads during his college playing days – from 2013-2015 with the Penn State Nittany Lions, he racked up 8,318 yards passing, 48 touchdowns, and a QB rating of 121.4. And he certainly caught the attention of Jets GM Mike Maccagnan, as Gang Green selected Hackenberg 51st overall (in the second round) in the 2016 NFL Draft.

So, what was so bad about Hackenberg's Jets career? Oh, only that he never played a *single regular season down* during his two-year stint with the team. Including 2016, where he was not even utilized during a wasted season (5-11) that saw Ryan Fitzpatrick benched for awful play, plus Geno Smith and Bryce Petty suffering season-ending injuries, nor 2017, where the team matched the previous year's record, and Hackenberg was inactive for much of the season (with Josh McCown and Petty carrying the heavy load).

After the season, Hackenberg was mercifully traded by the Jets to the Raiders, who eventually waived the QB…resulting in the trade being negated (only the Jets, right?)! After short stints with the

Eagles and Bengals (still never taking a snap in a regular season game for either), Hackenberg was drafted in 2019 by the Memphis Express of the short-lived Alliance of American Football (AAF), for whom he played in a total of three games, and netted such underwhelming stats as 277 yards, a lone TD (to three interceptions), and a QB rating of 43.6.

At the time of this book's release, Hackenberg was out of pro football completely, having taken a job as the quarterback coach for the Winslow Township High School football team, in New Jersey. And in case you were wondering – who did the Jets miss out on drafting when they selected Hackenberg in the 2016 NFL draft? Such subsequent Pro Bowlers as QB Dak Prescott and WR Tyreek Hill.

32

The QB With Kissing Disease

ACL issues, concussions, muscle pulls…all are common reasons for an NFL player to miss games during a season. Mononucleosis? *Not so much*. But the Jets have long enjoyed testing Murphy's law (i.e., "anything that can go wrong will go wrong"), and in 2019, Jets QB Sam Darnold missed three games due to mono – which, in all my years of being a spectator of professional sports, I honestly cannot recall a single time that I have heard of a player stricken with this ailment.

For those who are not familiar with mono, it is spread via saliva – most commonly through kissing, but also by sharing food utensils or a drinking glass with someone who is infected. And although usually not serious, such potential complications as swelling and/or rupturing of the spleen can arise.

It was never confirmed how Darnold acquired mono. All we know is he was diagnosed a few days after coming off an agonizing season opening choke loss to the Bills, 17-16 (a game the Jets were winning 16-0 in the 3rd quarter), and during the subsequent three games that Darnold was not spotted behind center, the position was temporarily filled ineffectively by either Trevor Siemian or Luke Falk.

I will give you a wild guess how many games they won in Darnold's absence. Of course, *zilch* – playing dead against the Browns (32-3), the Pats (30-14), and the Eagles (31-6) – which helped sink a once promising Jets season before it even began (which was Adam Gase's first as Jets HC). And to rub salt further into the wound, the Jets went 6-2 over their last eight games that year, so if it wasn't for Darnold's unexpected absence early on and taking a while to get back up to speed once returning, things could have turned out a whole lot different in 2019 (as the Jets finished with a 7-9 record).

31

The Bermuda Triangle for QB Talent

Bubby Brister. Browning Nagle. Brooks Bollinger. The Jets have certainly had their share of dud quarterbacks (and judging from the aforementioned list, a word to the wise – the Jets should stay away from any QB's whose name focuses heavily around the letter "B").

Admittedly, they've had one all-time great/Hall of Famer at the position (Joe Namath), as well as some that *almost* got the job done (Richard Todd, Ken O'Brien, Vinny Testaverde, Chad Pennington, Mark Sanchez, etc.), a few that reside in the "What if?" category (Matt Robinson, Ray Lucas, Jay Fiedler, Ryan Fitzpatrick, Sam Darnold, etc.), and those who enjoyed success elsewhere, but not nearly as much in a Jets uniform (Boomer Esiason, Neil O'Donnell, Brett Favre, Michael Vick, Joe Flacco, etc.).

But where would you classify such names as Christian Hackenberg, Rick Mirer, Glenn Foley, Frank Reich, Kellen Clemens, Greg McElroy, Bryce Petty, Luke Falk, Geno Smith, Jack Trudeau, Marty Domres, JJ Jones, Quincy Carter, Pat Ryan, Josh McCown, Kyle Mackey, Al Woodall, Bill Demory, Bob Davis, or Dick Wood?

Namath left the Jets after the 1976 season, and as of this book's release, the franchise is *still* waiting for a QB bold enough to truly fill his shoes…long-term.

30

Leon Takes Over

From the first year the Jets became *the Jets*, in 1963 (after going by the Titans moniker for three seasons prior), one of the team's co-owners was the founder of the Hess Corporation, Leon Hess – along with four other chaps (Sonny Werblin, Philip H. Iselin, Townsend B. Martin, and Donald Lillis).

Over the years, Hess bought out the other owners one by one, and on February 8, 1984, the last co-owner – Lillis' daughter, Helen Dillon – sold her share to Hess for an undisclosed amount. Although to get an idea of what an NFL team was worth at the time, Hess had bought out Martin's share several years prior for $5 million, a shockingly low figure when compared to the price tag of modern day NFL teams (in 2020, Forbes listed the Jets being valued at *$3.55 billion* – coming in 6th out of all 32 NFL franchises).

Did Hess becoming the sole owner help the team rise to the top? No, it did not. Quite the opposite, actually – during the time Hess was the Jets' sole owner (1984-1999), the team compiled an underwhelming record of 103-135, a head coach carousel would occur (including the misguided hiring of Rich Kotite, which led to some of the worst football in Jets history), and it was Hess' decision for the Jets to flee from New York to New Jersey.

Although to his credit, Hess was able to bring both Bill Parcells and Bill Belichick over from the Pats in 1997, which caused an immediate change in the team's fortunes (albeit briefly). Hess would pass away on May 7, 1999 at the age of 85 (from a blood disease), and ultimately, would not make good on a bold declaration he made a few years prior – "I'm 80 years old. I want results now."

29

Woody Takes Over

Ever since Leon Hess solely owned the Jets (from 1984 onward), for the most part, the team floundered. After his passing on May 7, 1999, the team was eventually put up for sale. And on January 11, 2000, billionaire Robert Wood Johnson IV – better known as Woody Johnson, and the heir to the Johnson & Johnson pharmaceutical fortune – won the right to purchase the Jets, for a cool $635 million.

At the time, Johnson issued a statement to the press concerning the purchase, that sounded promising to long-suffering Jets fans. "We want to emphasize that we are totally dedicated to bringing a winning and a championship team to this area. We understand and appreciate the difficulties inherent in that goal, but we look forward to working with Steve Gutman and Bill Parcells in developing a first-class organization, which is a cornerstone to developing a winning franchise."

Well, as of 2021, the Jets have failed to accomplish much, aside from qualifying for the playoffs in only four seasons, two trips to the AFC Championship Game, and a whole lotta losing (compiling a regular season record of 150 wins and 186 losses, albeit with Woody's brother, Christopher, taking over as CEO and acting owner from 2017-2021, while Woody served as the United States Ambassador to the United Kingdom during Donald Trump's presidency).

Obviously, Billy B. made the right choice to flee.

28

Riggins Runs Away

Fullback John Riggins put up some truly sparkling statistics as a member of the Jets from 1971-1975 (which was no mean feat, since the team was at best mediocre, at worst unwatchable during this time) – 3,880 yards rushing, becoming the first Jet in franchise history to rush for 1,000+ yards in a season (1,005 in 1975), setting a then-team record of 333 rushing yards in a single game (October 15, 1972 vs. the Pats), etc.

And behind only Broadway Joe, Riggins was one of the Jets' more flamboyant/unforgettable characters – whether it be sporting a mohawk, an afro, or painting his toenails green, he was impossible not to be seen. One small problem, Jets ownership of this era were, well, cheapskates – case in point, in his final year playing with the team, Riggins was paid *$63,000.* Understandably, he took the money and ran when he became a free agent in 1976 – signing with the Washington Redskins for $1.5 million over five years.

After sitting out all of 1980, Riggins returned to the 'Skins in 1981, and a year later, helped the team win Super Bowl XVII over the Jets' rival, the Dolphins, 27-17 (a game in which he rushed for a then-SB record of 166 yards, and was named SB MVP), and in 1992, was inducted into the Pro Football Hall of Fame.

But, back to '76 – rather than signing Riggins, the Jets had a worthy successor waiting in the wings to replace him, right? Of course not! It would be *another five years* until the Jets drafted Freeman McNeil.

27

Peyton Says "I'm Staying"

1997 showed great promise for the Jets. After the glum and gloomy Kotite era gave way to the bright and promising Parcells/Belichick era in February of that year, various newspapers were speculating that star college quarterback, Peyton Manning, was going to put the books down in favor of making the jump to the NFL. And wouldn't ya know it…the Jets possessed the #1 pick in the '97 NFL Draft.

But upon further contemplation, Manning opted to remain an extra season in college with the Tennessee Volunteers – and eventually deciding to go pro in '98, at which time, he signed on the dotted line with the Indianapolis Colts (resulting in a popular theory that Manning did this on purpose, as he simply did not want to play for the Jets, for whatever reason). Either way, the Jets once again had a close call with finally landing a worthy successor to Joe Namath…but came up short (Manning went on to have a Hall of Fame career with the Colts and Broncos, and winning a pair of Super Bowls along the way).

The Jets would wind up trading their place in line in the draft to the Rams – in exchange for the Rams' first, third, fourth and seventh round selections (which were #6, #67, #102, and #207). And it was proven once and for all that Manning truly *did* hate the Jets in 2019 – by personally calling Jets CEO, Christopher Johnson, and putting in a good word for the hiring of Adam Gase as the team's HC (as Gase was Manning's offensive coordinator with the Broncos for a spell).

26

The Colossal Collapse of 2000

The 2000 season is one of the more memorable in Jets' history…and unfortunately, not all for the right reasons. The first season since 1996 that their "savior," Bill Parcells, would not serve as their head coach (although he did occupy the GM position), Parcells' heir apparent, Bill Belichick, opted to flee rather than accept his new job title with the team. A largely unknown gent who ultimately proved to not be up to the high standard set by his predecessor was given the job, Al Groh.

But early in the season, there were genuine reasons for optimism – QB Vinny Testaverde (who had led the team to the 1998 AFC Championship Game, then missed almost the entire 1999 campaign with a ruptured Achilles tendon) was back behind the center, and the Jets jumped out to a strong 4-0 start (including a thrilling 21-17 week 4 victory over Keyshawn and the Bucs) before their week 5 bye.

And while there were stretches of poor play (a three-game losing streak in late October/early November), the season also included one of the greatest games in Jets' history, "The Monday Night Miracle," on October 23rd (in which the Jets came back against the Dolphins, from being beaten 30-7 in the 3rd quarter to eventually winning in OT, by a score of 40-37).

With the team sitting pretty with a 9-4 record entering the final three games of the season (after winning the last three consecutive games), not only did a playoff appearance seem like a forgone conclusion, but rather, a deep playoff run.

Oops.

Instead, the Jets opted to lose their last three games (including the final contest of the season on Christmas Eve to the year's eventual Super Bowl champs, the Baltimore Ravens, 34-20) – finishing the year at 9-7 and missing the playoffs entirely.

And as a bonus, Groh opted to go (exiting the Jets after a single season to take a job as the HC of a college team, the Virginia Cavaliers) – a mere six days after the season had been flushed down the toilet.

25

Gastineau's
Out-of-the-Blue Retirement

Going into the 1988 season, Mark Gastineau was seemingly on a clear path to the Hall of Fame. Although his on-field *and* off-field hijinks were sometimes hard to swallow (his "sack dance," his helmet winding up in Bernie Kosar's back, crossing the picket line of the 1987 player's strike, etc.), his numbers and accomplishments didn't lie.

Case in point, 67 career sacks (keep in mind, they only started counting sacks in 1982, which was Gastineau's fourth pro year), leading the NFL in sacks for two consecutive seasons ('83 and '84), five Pro Bowls, named the NEA NFL Defensive Player of the Year ('82), the UPI AFL-AFC Player of the Year ('84), etc.

But in '88, #99 began dating actress/Sylvester Stallone's ex-wife, Brigitte Nielsen, and on October 21st, shockingly announced he was abruptly retiring from football (in case you were wondering, he was still at the peak of his football powers – he was leading the AFC in sacks at the time). The reason? Gastineau claimed that Nielsen was diagnosed with cancer of the uterus…which the press shortly thereafter said it was a condition that, if left untreated, *might* have developed into cancer.

Either way, Gastineau was off the Jets, out of the NFL, and by 1990, done with his relationship with Nielsen.

24

Pennington's
Never-Ending Injuries

Another Jets blunder on draft day certainly occurred in 2000, when they selected Chad Pennington at the #18 spot overall, while some other geezer by the name of Tom Brady was drafted #199 (no, that's not a type-o...*#199*). But that said, if Pennington's career was not severely affected – and ultimately, shortened – by injuries, I (and I'm sure quite a few other Jets fans) am confident that he could have gone down as an all-time great, and possibly even returned the team to the Super Bowl, as evidenced by his leadership, talent, and intellect.

After mostly warming the bench during his first two seasons with the Jets, he was named starter in 2002, and eventually led the Jets to an AFC East Division Championship and even a playoff victory that year (a shocking thrashing of Peyton and the Colts, 41-0, in the Wild Card Round). Going into 2003, hopes ran high...until Pennington's first injury occurred – a fracture-dislocation on his left (non-throwing) hand after being hit by Giants linebacker Brandon Short in a preseason game, resulting in the QB missing significant time, and the Jets floundering to a 6-10 record.

In 2004, he injured his rotator cuff in a game vs. the Bills (resulting in three missed games), before returning and leading the Jets once again to the playoffs – which included a thrilling victory vs. the Chargers and then one of the most painful Jets playoff losses in team history (you'll read all about the gory details in the next entry).

After the season, Pennington underwent shoulder surgery (to repair the tear in his right rotator cuff and a bone spur), before again reinjuring his shoulder on September 25, 2005 in a game vs. the Jaguars, which resulted in yet another shoulder surgery, and the Jets subsequently skidding to a 4-12 record. Pennington came back strong in 2006 – leading the Jets to a playoff berth (losing to the Pats, 37-16, despite the QB passing for 300 yards) and winning the NFL's Comeback Player of the Year Award. However, all the injuries seemed to catch up to the QB in 2007, resulting in a sub-par season – which saw him benched in favor of Kellen Clemens.

And that's all she wrote for Pennington and the Jets – on August 7, 2008, the Jets acquired Brett Favre, and released Pennington that same day. Pennington would sign with the Dolphins, and wouldn't ya know it – he had a stellar year. Finishing with a passer rating of 97.4 and winning his second Comeback Player of the Year Award, Pennington led Miami to victory over his former team in the last game of the season to clinch the AFC East Division (before being promptly ousted by the Ravens in the first round of the playoffs, 27-9).

However, the injuries soon continued as a member of the Dolphins – including suffering another season-ending shoulder injury in a November 14, 2010 game vs. the Titans, and then, tearing his ACL on March 31, 2011, in a pick-up game of basketball – before announcing his retirement on February 9, 2012.

Certainly, James Chadwick Pennington will forever remain one of the Jets' biggest "What if?" questions.

23

All We Need
Is a Field Goal to Win, Doug

Funny how in professional sports, a player can go from hero to anti-hero in the blink of an eye. Or in the case of Jets placekicker, Doug Brien, a matter of *a week*. On January 8, 2005 against the San Diego Chargers in the Wild Card Round, Brien kicked the game-winning field goal (a 28-yarder) in OT, to give the Herman "You play to win the game" Edwards-coached Jets a hard-fought 20-17 victory – on the road. Up next, an even more daunting task – taking on the Pittsburgh Steelers at Heinz Field on January 15th, who just happened to have the best record in all of the NFL that year (15-1).

After the 1st quarter, the Black and Gold (led by rookie QB Ben Roethlisberger) led Gang Green (led by Chad Pennington), 10-0. But then, a funny thing happened – the Jets somehow *outplayed* the Steelers for the next two quarters, and had built a surprising 17-10 lead going into the 4th quarter. The Steelers managed to tie it in the 4th, but the Jets refused to lose their cool – instead, responding immediately after with a drive that reached Pittsburgh's 30-yard line, with two minutes left on the clock.

It was Brien's time to shine once again with a 47-yard field goal attempt to put the Jets ahead. *Miss #1* (the ball appeared to be doing the right thing, before bouncing off the crossbar and not going through). On the very next play, the Steelers appeared to have given the game away to the Jets, when Big Ben threw a pick, and

Brien was quickly given a kick at redemption. After eating time off the clock by Pennington taking a knee, Brien attempted a 43-yarder with 4 seconds left. *Miss #2* (sailing wide left).

The game then went to OT, and despite the Jets winning the coin toss, failed to score and wound up punting, before the Steelers put the Jets out of their misery when Jeff Reed showed Brien how it's done, and successfully kicked a 33-yard field goal.

Perhaps sensing fans' potential displeasure towards Brien, he would never play another game for the Jets – going over to the Chicago Bears the next season, before retiring. At the time of this book's release, Brien ranks at an impressive #56 on the "NFL Field Goal Percentage Career Leaders List," with an 80.233% mark.

Too bad that percentage readout does not include *one specific extra field goal.*

Final score: Steelers 20, Jets 17.

22

Dangers of the Game

Admittedly, this entry is not directed solely at the Jets, but rather, *the entire NFL*. Since football is a high-contact sport, players are constantly at risk for injury. But looking back, there is no denying the NFL's poor handling of concussions suffered by players over the years (particularly before better protocol and diagnosis was put in place circa the early 21st century). The amount of players from the '60s, '70s, '80s, and '90s (and undoubtedly also earlier) who suffered from not just a concussion at some point in their career – but rather, *multiple* concussions – is staggering.

And not to mention, many of the players continued to play on in spite of the injury – resulting in debilitating aftereffects that continued and seemed to worsen after their playing days were over (particularly, the sad/tragic tales of Junior Seau, Andre Waters, and Mike Webster, among many others).

And while quite a few Jets players suffered from head injuries during their playing career (Wayne Chrebet, Wesley Walker, Joe Namath, etc.), one that perhaps stands out the most is WR Al Toon. Toon seemed to be on his way to a Hall of Fame caliber career early on, before he suffered at least nine (!) concussions during eight seasons, from 1985-1992, which forced his retirement at age 29.

When I interviewed Toon for the book *Sack Exchange,* I asked "If anything could have been different with how the Jets' staff handled Toon's concussions." He replied, "Sure – hindsight's always 20/20. There's been more research done. And I think today, maybe things would have been handled a little differently. But back then they asked my opinion – how did I feel. It wasn't just the medical staff that made the decision – they asked me how I felt. So I was partly to blame too, in going back out to play on the field maybe too soon."

Still, you can't help but wonder what could have been done differently over the years concerning helping protect football players when it came to concussions. Plus, how many players could have had not only better/longer careers, but not suffered from the consequences after retirement – particularly, from CTE/chronic traumatic encephalopathy (brain degeneration likely caused by repeated head traumas).

Concerning the overall safety/health of players, the Jets have been lucky to mostly avoid another danger – spinal cord injuries. As of this book's arrival, it has only happened once in Jets history – when DE Dennis Byrd collided with DL Scott Mersereau against the Chiefs on November 29, 1992. Byrd broke his fifth cervical vertebrae and it was thought that he would be paralyzed.

However, Byrd eventually was able to walk again (through physical therapy) and even attended the Jets' home opener the following season – but never played another game. Mersereau would play one more season, when it was discovered that he had suffered three cracked vertebrae (which he believes occurred during his collision with Byrd, but was not properly diagnosed). Sadly, Byrd would die in an auto accident on October 15, 2016, at the age of 50 (four years after the Jets retired his #90).

When I interviewed Walker (who required spinal fusion surgery after his playing days were over) for *Long Island Pulse* in 2016, I asked, "Would you recommend playing football as a career?" He replied, "As a parent, I don't know if I would let my kids play the game...I would let them play, because it's their decision. But I'd try to steer them in another direction. Because you don't even know, you can just land the wrong way and hit your head and that could change your whole life."

21

Jets Head Coach #21

After four disappointing seasons under head coach Todd Bowles (including his final campaign in which the Jets finished a measly 4-12), it was most certainly time for a change. As expected, Bowles was fired on December 30, 2018. And with Super Bowl-winning former Green Bay Packers coach Mike McCarthy unemployed and available to serve as Bowles' replacement (MM appeared keen on the potential position – even landing a job interview with Gang Green), this would be a no-brainer/slam-dunk, right?

Come on, this is *the Jets*!

Instead of going with proven winner McCarthy, the Jets went with…Adam Gase. Wait. *What*?! Yes, that "Adam Gase" that was just fired by the Dolphins after three seasons and compiling a subpar 23-25 record.

Supposedly, Gase's pal, Peyton Manning (Gase served as the Broncos' offensive coordinator during Manning's stellar 2013 season), personally spoke to the Jets' higher-ups and praised Gase. In case you were wondering, yes, this was indeed *the same Peyton Manning* that opted to go back to college for one more year to avoid being drafted first overall by the Jets in 1997.

Either way, the phone call only increased the speed of the wheels being put in motion for Gase's hiring – which soon became official, to the shock of Jets fans. Although perhaps the most flabbergasted was sports radio personality Joe Benigno (the next time you have some time to kill, search YouTube for some of the classic Benigno anti-Gase rants from 2019 and 2020 – they're quite entertaining).

Perhaps fans should have known not all was kosher from the press conference announcing Gase's hiring on January 14, 2019, when the Jets' new HC's crazed-looking eyes stole the show and became the talk of the sports world. And it all went downhill from there – a 7-9 record in 2019 (don't let the record fool you, they were 1-7 at one point) and a horrifically bad 2-14 record in 2020 (in which the sad sack team didn't win their first game until week 15, and set a new franchise record for most consecutive losses, with 13).

And let's not forget that during the "Gase era," once-promising QB Sam Darnold floundered, big name free agent Le'Veon Bell was signed, underperformed (not entirely his fault, thanks to his *un*-supporting cast), and only stayed with the team for a season plus two games, and Pro Bowler Jamal Adams was traded.

Thankfully, the Jets would give Gase the old-heave-ho on January 3, 2021 – replacing him with former 49ers defensive coordinator, Robert Saleh.

And in case you were wondering what became of the HC that the Jets fired before the Gase hire, Todd Bowles was hired as defensive coordinator of the Buccaneers...and almost immediately made Tampa Bay one of the top defenses in the NFL (culminating in a Super Bowl LV victory, in which the Bucs' D stifled the explosive Chiefs' O, 31-9).

20

Jets Head Coach #12

Want to give any long-time Jets fan heartburn? Just mention "Rich Kotite." The Jets have had a few dandy bad coaches in their history, but Kotite takes the cake (which is no small feat – especially after the stench that Adam Gase left behind in 2020). Previously serving as the Jets' wide receivers coach (1983-1984) and offensive coordinator (1985-1989), Kotite enjoyed some success as the head coach of the Philadelphia Eagles (10-6 in 1991 and 11-5 in 1992), before floundering (8-8 in 1993 and 7-9 in 1994) and getting fired.

The Jets had just fired Pete Carroll after a single season (in which they finished 6-10) and were in need of a new leader – which resulted in the Jets not only naming Kotite their HC, but also (unbelievably), their general manager for his second year, as well. What followed was not only two horrific seasons (3-15 in 1995 and 1-15 in 1996), but also, he was one the masterminds behind one of the Jets' biggest draft blunders of all-time – selecting Kyle Brady over eventual Hall of Famer Warren Sapp in '95.

Mercifully, Kotite exited the team on December 20, 1996, but in a truly "Kotite-ian" fashion – *he fired himself* (remember, he was also the GM at the time). Thankfully, Leon Hess brought in "The Bills" (Parcells and Belichick), and all was right in the Jets' world from a leadership position…at least until January 4, 2000.

19

6-Year Contract as HC…
Gone After 3

When Bill Parcells was named Jets' head coach in 1997, automatically, it made the team who had long been an NFL laughingstock one to be taken seriously. *Very seriously.* Signed to a 6-year contract as "chief of football operations," within three years' time, the Jets narrowly missed a playoff appearance twice ('97 and '99) and one season in which they almost made it to the Super Bowl ('98). Of course, Parcells would want to return and finish the job for year four, right?

Wrong.

On January 3, 2000, Parcells opted to step down as the Jets' head coach, but, stay on as general manager. OK, fine. With Bill Belichick waiting – and well-groomed – to inherit the head coaching job from Parcells, the Jets would be in good hands, and the change would be seamless, right? Ha! Instead of spoiling the surprise here, I'll give you a hint – it is analyzed in all its dreadful details as one of the top picks of this book (come on, I can't spoil the surprise and tell you *exactly* which #).

It was never explained fully as to why the man many refer to as the "Big Tuna" or simply "Tuna" (at a 1997 press conference, Parcells described the origin of the odd nickname as "There was an old commercial from StarKist with Charlie the StarKist tuna. So my players were trying to con me on something one time, and I said,

'You must think I'm Charlie the Tuna,' you know, a sucker") decided to abruptly step down as head coach from the Jets. And when you take into consideration that he would later resurface as the head coach of the Cowboys from 2003-2006 – where he had less power than with the Jets (heavy-handed owner Jerry Jones also served as GM of America's Team) – the move remains a bit bewildering.

Either way, although Parcells did succeed in getting the Jets back on track, he did *not* complete the job (getting the Jets to finally become 2x Super Bowl champs).

Ta-ta, Tuna.

18

We Just Need to Hold This Lead For 2 More Quarters to Make It to the Super Bowl (Part I)

In the history of the NFL, few teams made as quick a turnaround as the Jets from 1996-1998. In case you forgot, the Jets endured their worst season ever in '96 (going 1-15 in the final year of the dingy "Kotite era"), before Bill Parcells swooped in to save the day – finishing 9-7 in '97 and narrowly missing the playoffs, before taking first place in the AFC East in '98. And after the Jets had their way with the Jaguars in the Divisional Round that year, 34-24, they were graciously invited by defending SB champs, the Broncos, to play against them in the AFC Championship Game at Mile High Stadium.

Understandably, the Broncos were favored to win the whole enchilada. But seemingly, the Jets never received the memo – they actually went into halftime winning by a slim 3-0 margin, before Jets tight end Blake Spence blocked a punt in the 3rd quarter that was recovered on the 1-yard line, and then, Curtis Martin scampered in for a TD on the next play. So, now with a 10-0 lead and momentum clearly on the Jets' side, they should be able to build upon this fortunate turn of events, right?

Wrong.

The Jets merely awoke a snoozing beast. The Broncos promptly put up 23 unanswered points (some "highlights" including John Elway throwing a 47-yard bomb to Ed McCaffery, and on a kickoff, the ball getting caught up in the Mile High wind which led to the Broncos recovering the ball…only the Jets, right?).

Lastly, how the heck could Vinny Testaverde end up with 356 yards passing (albeit, because of a horrible running game that day – Martin finished with just 14 rushing yards – Vinny had no other choice), and the Jets *still* lose?

Somehow, they found a way.

Final score: Broncos 23, Jets 10.

17

We Just Need to Hold This Lead For 2 More Quarters to Make It to the Super Bowl (Part II)

Ever since the 1972 Miami Dolphins became the only NFL team to ever finish a season completely undefeated (going 17-0, including a Super Bowl VII victory), several teams have flirted with also going undefeated…but at the time of this book's release, all have come up short.

And one such powerhouse team that was in the running for much of the season to match the '72 Dolphins was the 2009 Indianapolis Colts. Led by Peyton Manning, the Colts were sitting pretty with a 14-0 record, when it seemed that HC Jim Caldwell opted to have his team take the foot off the gas pedal, and take it easy for the last two games of the regular season – to ensure that his starters were in tip-top shape for the playoffs.

And by opting for this maneuver – much to the chagrin of most Colt fans, as the team had a golden opportunity to make history – they dropped the last two games, to the Jets (29-15) and to the Bills (30-7). But the Colts hit the ground running in the playoffs – by kicking the Ravens' keysters in the Divisional Round, 20-3. The Colts' opponent in the AFC Championship Game? The New York Jets (who proved to be a pleasant surprise in the playoffs that year, beating the Bengals in the Wild Card, 24-14, and then the Chargers in the Divisional, 17-14).

The Colts were understandably favored, but a funny thing happened during the first half of the AFC Championship in Indy...*the Jets outplayed the Colts*. In fact, at one point late in the 2nd quarter, the Jets had constructed a 17-6 lead (and could have had even more, if not for a missed Jay Feely field goal attempt early on).

However, the Colts eventually awoke (flashbacks of the '99 AFC Championship Game, anyone?), scoring a touchdown before the half, and then completely dominating the Jets in the second half. In fact, Gang Green didn't score a single stinking point the entire second half of the game.

Final score: Colts 30, Jets 17.

16

Too Little, Too Late

After coming off what is probably the biggest non-1968 playoff win in franchise history – a thrilling 28-21 triumph over Belichick, Brady, and the Pats in the 2010 Divisional Round…*in Foxborough* – the only thing standing between the Jets and Super Bowl XLV was the Pittsburgh Steelers. All signs pointed to a Jets victory – they had already beaten the Steelers earlier in the season on the road (22-17), both of their playoff victories that year had been on the road, and this would be their second AFC Championship Game appearance in a row.

So, they would be better prepared than their previous year's half-awake/half-asleep showing, correct? Incorrect. It appeared as though the Jets were severely hungover from the high of the previous week, as the Steelers jumped out to a commanding 24-0 lead just before half-time, before a Nick Folk field goal made it 24-3 at the half.

Then…the Jets borrowed a page from the "Same Old Jets handbook" – particularly, the 1981 Wildcard – and mounted a *furious* comeback. And momentum was clearly on the Jets' side midway through the 4th quarter when down 24-10, the Jets had a golden first-and-goal opportunity on the Steelers' 2-yard line…and wound up not getting *a single* point.

But the Jets refused to die quietly – a safety on Steelers QB Ben Roethlisberger made it 24-12, and then a 4-yard TD pass from Sanchez to Jerricho Cotchery and a Folk extra point made it 24-19 with just over three minutes to play. Then, the Jets season came down to one play – they needed to stop the Steelers on a 3rd and 6 on their 40-yard line (with under 2 minutes to go and 0 timeouts left). Unfortunately, Roethlisberger and Antonio Brown had other plans – connecting on a 14-yard catch, and then, running out the clock.

JSO – "Jets Season Over."

As previously mentioned in this book's intro, most Jets fans (myself included) assumed that with back-to-back AFC Championship Game appearances, the Ryan/Sanchez tandem would only improve and eventually lead the Jets to the promised land. Oh, how wrong we were – as of this book's release (2021), this would mark the Jets' last playoff appearance.

Final score: Steelers 24, Jets 19.

15

The Flying Lawnmower

This entry is one of the truly tragic – and unfathomable – events in Jets history. The safety of spectators at any public event should be first and foremost on the organizers' minds, right? Well, the Jets' management failed to overlook this key factor during a halftime show on December 9, 1979 at Shea Stadium, in a game vs. the Patriots (that the Jets would win, 27-26).

A show put on by the Electronic Eagles of the Radio Control Association of Greater New York consisted of radio-controlled airplanes that sailed around the stadium – including unwisely not solely keeping their path of flight to over the vacated football field, but having them also fly over the crowd. And one of the odder contraptions on exhibit that day was a two-foot plane called the Flying Lawnmower (because…it was shaped like a lawnmower).

Operated by an auto collision repairman named Philip Cushman, the object (mostly made of metal) crashed into the audience five rows behind from where the Patriots' bench was located, striking 20-year-old John Bowen in the head (who would later die from a brain injury) and 25-year-old Kevin Rourke (who sustained a concussion).

The New York Times would later report on November 18, 1981 that a $10 million federal lawsuit was filed by Bowen's father, James, which named the New York Jets Football Club, the Radio Control Association of Greater New York, and Philip Cushman as defendants. The outcome of the lawsuit could not be located.

14

Goodbye Shea, Hello NJ

Beginning in 1964, the Jets called Shea Stadium home. And while the stadium located in Flushing, Queens certainly saw its share of Jets highlights (the 1968 American Football League Championship Game, Namath's riveting near-comeback win vs. the 49ers in 1971, the playoff-clinching final game of the 1981 season, etc.), it was never fully *their* stadium.

As seen by its design, it was built for baseball (the Jets co-inhabited Shea with the Mets) – most obviously with how the field was not completely encircled by permanent seats, as most football stadiums are. But still, the Jets occupied Shea for many years (and was super-convenient to get to – via the Long Island Railroad and the Subway having a stop right there, and the Long Island Expressway/I-495 being an easily accessible driving route).

But according to former Jets director of operations, Tim Davey, in the *Sack Exchange* book, Leon Hess had had enough by 1983. "They didn't move a muscle, the city – because they had no money. They wouldn't do anything at that stadium. If it came down to getting something done at the stadium and the city was not going to do it, I would take it off the rent. Whether it was a renovation job in the locker room – which we did – all sorts of different things. Improvements. But his biggest thing was cleaning up the stadium, one. And two, cleaning up the bathrooms. I mean, we had patrons coming in to our offices with soiled jackets, that they sent to testing, that came back with urine on it – from the pipes up above them, that were leaking! Leon knew about this. The funny thing is that Shea Stadium never renovated or had any work done to it until after we left. That's when they started renovating and started putting in all private boxes, and cleaning up the place really well."

While there were rumblings that Jets' ownership wasn't overjoyed with how they were being treated at Shea – particularly Hess – it didn't seem *that* serious of a threat that they would leave, especially with the franchise seemingly experiencing a renaissance in the early '80s. But a little-known fact that was not made all that public at the time was that the Jets' 20-year lease was up at the end of '83. So, seemingly out of nowhere, it was announced mid-season that the Jets would be leaving Shea after '83, after the city (or specifically, mayor Ed Koch, who seemed more a baseball fan than a football fan) did diddly to try and convince the Jets otherwise.

The next question was, "Where would they go?" Up to this point, one "comeback remark" that Jets fans held in their back pocket while debating Giants fans was that the Jets remained a *true* New York football team...whereas the Giants had called New Jersey their home since 1976 (but retained the "New York" in their name).

But beginning in 1984, Jets fans could no longer flaunt that claim...the Jets would be *sharing* Giants Stadium with the Giants.

13

"Same Old Jets"

There are certain nicknames that you would *not* want linked to a professional sports franchise – Dem Bums (the Brooklyn Dodgers), Bungles (the Cincinnati Bengals), the Flaming Snot Donkeys (Calgary Flames), etc. And fans of the New York Jets are unfortunately quite familiar with the oft-used phrase "Same Old Jets." Now, that said, such a phrase could have been used as a compliment if it first reared its head, oh say, late in the 1969 season – as in, "The Same Old Jets…they just clinched another playoff spot and look poised to win back-to-back Super Bowls."

But unfortunately, "SOJ" seemed to first rear its head sometime in the '80s or '90s, after year after year of frustrating, agonizing, and/or mind-boggling blunders, brain-farts, and choke-jobs. For example, "The Same Old Jets…they drafted Kyle Brady instead of Warren Sapp." "The Same Old Jets…they seemingly fell asleep in the second half of the 2009 AFC Championship Game." "The Same Old Jets…they committed a Butt Fumble on national TV on Thanksgiving evening."

The list is infinite, I'm afraid.

And lastly, a special shout-out to a few rib-tickling Jets-related acronyms that long-time fans know all too well – "**J**ust **E**nd **T**he **S**eason" and "**J**ust **E**ndure **T**he **S**uffering."

12

Our Coach Just Led Us To the AFC Championship Game. Let's Get Rid of Him!

As the defensive coordinator of the Jets from 1963-1972, Walt Michaels played a major role in the '69 squad that held the mighty Baltimore Colts to a single touchdown (scored late in the 4th quarter, by the way) in Super Bowl III. But when he was not selected to replace Weeb Ewbank as the Jets' head coach following the '72 season (the position would go to Ewbank's *son in law*, Charley Winner), Michaels left and was employed for the next three seasons by the Philadelphia Eagles as their DC.

After lackluster results with Winner, the Jets welcomed Michaels back as DC for the '76 season, before – finally – naming him their head coach for '77. Several up and down seasons followed, before ultimately delivering in '81 – with the Jets' first trip to the playoffs since '69. But the strike-shortened '82 season would be Michaels' finest – finishing 6-3, blowing out reigning AFC Champs the Cincinnati Bengals 44-17 in the Wild Card Round, and winning a thriller against the Los Angeles Raiders 17-14 in the Divisional Round...*both on the road.*

But as you'll soon read in entry #6, the Jets' '82 season came to a sad end when they were beaten in Miami on a soggy and sloppy field, in the AFC Championship, 14-0 (aka, "The Mud Bowl").

Obviously, the Jets had vastly improved in '81 and '82 (after handing in either mediocre or downright stinky seasons from 1970-1980) and Michaels' players played hard for him and respected him – particularly the Jets' fearsome Sack Exchange. So, what did the Jets do shortly after their first trip to a Championship Game in over a decade…grant Michaels more power within the organization? Generously rework his contract and offer an extension? Reward him with a brand new Cadillac?

According to people close to the team at the time, he was *forced* into retirement.

So, why exactly was the then-53-year-old Michaels no longer the Jets' coach? In a UPI news article dated February 9, 1983 (simply titled *Michaels Resigns as Jets' Coach*), Michaels was quoted as saying "I have spent 32 years in this game and I've enjoyed them all. But in that time, I have never taken a vacation and have never spent enough time with my family. Now I think it's time that I should, so I am retiring as head coach of the Jets effective Tuesday, February 8, 1983. I wish my assistant coaches, the players and the rest of the organization and the next head coach good luck in the future."

Rumors have surfaced over the years that Michaels was an alcoholic or addicted to pain killers, which he himself addressed in the *Sack Exchange* book. "There were a lot of accusations made – oh, I was a drug addict and I was an alcoholic. But do you know who the alcoholics were? That's for you to research. I would not say that or accuse anyone of anything, because that's not my personality. I had all of those tests taken. I was not either one – alcoholic or drug-addicted. The rest of it, they went their way and I went my way. There are so many ways that there were people wrong – including people in the league office."

The Jets' offensive coordinator, Joe Walton, was named their new HC, but the team chemistry was never the same. "It's unfortunate that the Jets got rid of him when they did, because we were on the way to the Super Bowl – to be perennial Super Bowl Champions," former Jets offensive tackle Chris Ward said in the *Sack Exchange* book. "I really do believe that. I really believe they should have kept Walt Michaels – every year, we were going a game or two farther in the playoffs. The team that we had was not old. We were one or two players away from being perennial Super Bowl Champions. We had the makings of it – we had a great offensive line, a great defensive line, skilled positions. Some of them could have been better, but it didn't really matter – we won by running the ball and maintaining that by playing good defense. I really hated to see Walt Michaels go. I really believe that it was a slide for the Jets."

Ward was not kidding when he said the Jets experienced a "slide" after Michaels's exit. Fans had to wait three more years for the team to reach the playoffs again, and an additional *16 more years* to participate in another AFC Championship Game. Even more befuddling was that after Michaels came out of retirement and coached the New Jersey Generals of the USFL for two seasons, 1984 and 1985 (and making the playoffs both times), he was never given another NFL coaching job – before passing away at the age of 89, on July 10, 2019.

11

No to Marino

Admittedly, it's easy to look back – years later – and question why certain players were not drafted over others in the NFL. After all, for every slam dunk draft pick (Peyton Manning, Terry Bradshaw, Bruce Smith, etc.), there have been countless misfires (Ryan Leaf, JaMarcus Russell, Akili Smith, etc.). But that said, Jets fans have understandably been asking themselves for decades, "Why oh why did the Jets draft Ken O'Brien instead of Dan Marino?"

In the 1983 draft, the Jets (who were one of the NFL's top teams at the time, having just reached the AFC Championship Game three months earlier) landed at #24 in the first round. So, when their time came, they opted to choose a player who did put up good stats in college (heck, he'd even enter the College Football Hall of Fame in 1997), Ken O'Brien, out of California-Davis.

Fair enough.

But why O'Brien was chosen while Marino was still available – a player who proved to be a winner while with the Pittsburgh Panthers (of the University of Pittsburgh), leading the team to a Sugar Bowl victory in 1982 and a tough loss the following year in the Cotton Bowl – is an absolute mind-boggler.

Some say it was because Marino's stock had fallen due to a not-so-great senior year and/or rumors of recreational drug use (which concerning the latter, has never been confirmed as fact). As Jets HC Joe Walton recounted in the *Sack Exchange* book, "Dan

Marino was not on our board. When we got ready for the draft, there were some rumors about things about Dan that I wasn't aware of. I knew what a good player he was, but we had a very strict drafting procedure, and there were certain people we were not allowed to draft – for one reason or another. We thought Ken O'Brien was a guy that would fit into our offense very well."

Once O'Brien and Marino both hit the pros, it quickly became apparent that the Jets had most certainly fumbled the ball – with Marino taking his Dolphins to the Super Bowl in just his second year and embarking on a Hall of Fame career. Admittedly, O'Brien did have flashes of greatness during his ten-year NFL career…but nowhere near the talent, success, nor leadership of the man the Jets passed on.

10

Season Over In
Opening Game's 2nd Quarter

The 1998 Jets provided fans with undoubtedly one of the franchise's greatest seasons ever – going 12-4 and falling just short of a trip to Super Bowl XXXIII (due to their defeat by the eventual Super Bowl champs, the Denver Broncos, in the AFC Championship). And it was a near *miraculous* turnaround if you think that just two seasons ago, they finished a putrid 1-15.

So understandably, expectations ran high entering the 1999 season. Especially, with Bill Parcells *and* Bill Belichick returning for their third seasons as the Jets' respective head coach and defensive coordinator. And also, the season would serve as Vinny Testaverde's first full one as the Jets' QB (who was a major reason for the team's success the previous season). A "can't miss" opportunity, right?

Wrong.

In the second quarter of the opening game of the 1999 season on September 12th – a home game against the New England Patriots – the usually sure-handed running back Curtis Martin fumbled (and then recovered) the ball. Nothing too out of the ordinary…except that Testaverde (who was not touched during the play) would not play another snap that season, as he had ruptured his Achilles tendon after taking a single step in the direction of where the fumble occurred. It was later blamed on the dastardly AstroTurf of

Giants Stadium for causing the injury (unlike regular grass, AstroTurf had seams, which can lead to twisted knees).

Either way, the game – and the remainder of the season, for that matter – still had to be played. Only one problem – a gamble by Parcells failed to pay off. For reasons unknown, he had listed punter Tom Tupa as the #2 quarterback and Rick Mirer as the #3 "emergency" quarterback – leaving Ray Lucas inactive. So, here's the catch – since Mirer was deemed the emergency QB, he was not permitted to play until the start of the 4th quarter, or else, Tupa could no longer participate in the game (not even as a punter).

So, Tupa was forced into double duty (with the score Patriots 10, Jets 7), and it looked like this whacky move may pay off – he immediately fired a 25-yard TD to Keyshawn Johnson, and put up respectable stats, which included going 6-10 for 165 yards and two TD's. But after Tupa fumbled the ball and the Pats recovered it for a TD (and a 17-16 lead) early in the 3rd quarter, it became crystal clear that the Jets would be turning to Mirer for the 4th quarter.

Turns out they could have just stuck with Tupa for the rest of the game – halfway through the 4th quarter, the Jets were ahead, 28-27, after LB Bryan Cox returned an interception for a TD (but the 2-point conversion failed). And then…*the killer* – Mirer was intercepted by Pats LB Chris Slade as the game was winding down, ultimately resulting in an Adam Vinatieri field goal with just three seconds left in the game, and, a Jets loss.

How did the Jets fare in the wake of this opening day disaster, you ask? Not well, I'm afraid (in case you forgot, I suggest you go back and consult entry #46 for a refresher).

Shortly after the game and Vinny's season-ending injury, it was announced that Giants Stadium would be using natural grass the following year. Too bad that change from AstroTurf to grass didn't occur *before* September 12, 1999.

Final score: Patriots 30, Jets 28.

9

Denied Shot at
Super Bowl Repeat

At the end of the regular season in 1969, the Jets qualified for the playoffs (finishing first in the AFL Eastern Division with a 10-4 record) and were set to host the Divisional Playoff Round at home against the Kansas City Chiefs. And with Broadway Joe still in full effect (before injuries became constant) and the Jets coming off a simply iconic Super Bowl victory the year before, momentum appeared to be on their side – despite having been trounced by the Chiefs in week 10, 34-16.

Taking place on Saturday, December 20th, blustery winds and a chilly 33°F temp made it not exactly the most cozy game to attend at old Shea, and the conditions resulted in three missed field goals by KC kicker Jan Stenerud.

And by the 4th quarter, it appeared to be anybody's game with the Chiefs clinging on to a slim 6-3 lead…until KC defensive back Emmitt Thomas was flagged for pass interference in the end zone, resulting in the Jets being gifted the ball on the KC 1-yard line. Surely, out of three tries, the Jets would score a TD.

Negative.

Two runs and one pass attempt led nowhere, which resulted in the Jets having to settle for a Jim Turner field goal to tie the game. And wouldn't ya know it, on the Chiefs' next possession, Len Dawson completed a 61-yard strike to Otis Taylor, and a short while later, hooked up with Gloster Richardson in the end zone – resulting in what would turn out to be a Chiefs victory (Dawson and co. would go on to defeat the Raiders in the AFL Championship, 17-7, before upsetting the Vikings in Super Bowl IV, 23-7).

What really killed the Jets in the game was the performance of their eventual Hall of Fame QB – Namath completed just 14 of 40 passes (for 169 yards) and no TD's, and was intercepted *three times*. But with Namath still young (26 years old at the time), two back-to-back winning seasons/playoff qualifications, and the aforementioned SB win in '69, one would assume that the Jets would continue cruising to success throughout the '70s, correct?

Incorrect.

The loss would lead to an excruciating stretch of the franchise not getting a whiff of the playoffs for more than a decade (1981).

Final score: Chiefs 13, Jets 6.

8

The Marathon by the Lake

The Jets' 1986 regular season started out splendidly…then turned into an absolute horror show (remember entry #37?). But miraculously, they still somehow managed to qualify for the playoffs, and even stopped the bleeding with a much-needed victory in the Wild Card Round, by blowing out the Chiefs, 35-15, at home.

And the momentum of the win seemed to carry over into the next game – the Divisional Round, against the Browns in Cleveland, on January 3, 1987. In a game that is now best-known as "The Marathon by the Lake" (the Browns' then-home, Cleveland Stadium, was situated close to Lake Erie), it appeared as though the Jets had a victory sealed up after a 25-yard Freeman McNeil TD run made it Jets 20, Browns 10, with only 4 minutes remaining in regulation. Heck, Jets broadcaster Charley Steiner even went as far as euphorically declaring, "The Jets are going to win this football game! The Jets are going to the AFC Championship!"

But instead, the team offered up a superb display of the infamous saying, "snatching defeat from the jaws of victory." The Jets D had the Browns O pinned all the way back on the home team's 18 yard line, and on a 2nd and 24, Cleveland QB Bernie Kosar had his pass batted down. Here comes 3rd down, right? Not so fast. Jets DE Mark Gastineau drilled Kosar in the back with his helmet well after he had thrown the pass – resulting in a *killer* roughing the passer penalty.

You can probably guess what happened next – the Browns promptly went on to tie the game in regulation, and took the game into overtime. And it took *two quarters of overtime* for a winner to be declared – with Browns kicker Mark Moseley ultimately hitting a 27-yard field goal (after missing a 23-yarder earlier in OT), and presenting Jets fans with quite possibly the most painful/shocking loss in franchise history.

Final score: Browns 23, Jets 20.

7

The Heidi Game

Going into week 11 of the 1968 regular season, the Jets were flying high with a 7-2 record (and a four-game winning streak), and were set to face one of the AFL's other top teams, the Oakland Raiders – who enjoyed the same record as Joe Namath and company – at Oakland-Alameda County Coliseum, on November 17th.

And it proved to be an exciting contest entering the 4th quarter – with a score of Raiders 22, Jets 19. And the excitement continued throughout the final quarter for TV viewers (especially if you were a Jets fan) – with a little more than a minute left on the clock, the score was Jets 32, Raiders 29, after a 26-yard field goal by Jim Turner. And then…something happened that (go ahead, fill in the rest of the sentence) could *only* happen to the Jets.

The TV network that was broadcasting the game, NBC, was set to show a made-for-TV film of the classic children's novel, *Heidi* (starring Jennifer Edwards in the lead role), at 7pm EST. Nowadays, if a sporting event is going to run over its allotted time, it is a forgone conclusion that there will be an announcement that the next program will start once the game ends. But I guess TV programmers were more stupid back in 1968, as a decision was made to cut away from the game to start *Heidi* on time – with just over a minute left to play in this close contest.

And wouldn't ya know it, the Jets promptly choked the game away – Raiders QB Daryle Lamonica threw a 43-yard pass to running back Charlie Smith to make it 36-32, before Jets punt returner Earl

Christy fumbled the ensuing kickoff (with 42 seconds remaining) and Oakland reserve running back Preston Ridlehuber recovered the ball and ran it into the end zone. But at least the geniuses at NBC were kind enough to flash a message of "SPORTS BULLETIN: RAIDERS DEFEAT JETS 43-32" during the broadcast of *Heidi*.

This broadcasting snafu – now commonly referred to as "The Heidi Game" – led to networks that televise sporting events finally getting wise and letting games finish before starting the next scheduled program.

But to the Jets' credit, they did not "pull a Same Old Jets" and use this horrific loss as an excuse to then let their season disappear into the abyss. Instead, the Jets immediately bounced back and won the remaining four games of the season – to finish in first place in the AFL Eastern Division (with an 11-3 record), exact revenge on the Raiders in the AFL Championship Game (winning 27-23), before Namath "guaranteed" and delivered victory in Super Bowl III.

Final score: Raiders 43, Jets 32.

6

The Mud Bowl

In the strike-shortened 1982-83 season, the Jets finished at 6-3 – coming in second in the AFC East (just a single game behind the Dolphins). Earning a return trip to the playoffs, the Jets then enjoyed two surprising road victories – a blowout in the Wildcard Round over the Bengals (44-17) and a thriller in the Divisional Round over the Raiders (17-14).

The only thing that now stood between the Jets and a ticket to Super Bowl XVII would be a meet-up with their old pals, the Dolphins, in the AFC Championship at the Orange Bowl Game, on January 23, 1983. And after coming up short against the Fins in their two regular season meetings (including a nail-bitter in week 7 that was decided in the final seconds by a winning field goal, 20-19), it seemed like the Jets were primed for some sweet revenge.

But Mother Nature had other plans.

When I interviewed Frank Ramos (the Jets' director of public relations from 1963-2002) for *Sack Exchange*, he explained what happened from his perspective – "It had been raining in Miami since Wednesday afternoon. They were still watering, rather than the pump taking water off the field. When our players went on the field, the water was over the top of your shoes for the players. Walt was blaming it on Shula, but the game was supposed to be handled by the National Football League – they were supposed to be in charge of the Championship Game and the conditions."

"And they had done nothing about it. And the Orange Bowl did not own a tarp. There was not a tarp on the field for all those days, and the Orange Bowl – at that time – throughout the season, high school football played there two to three games a week. Plus the University of Miami and the Dolphins played. The field could not handle that type of water, because the grass had really been chewed up throughout the season."

What occurred was what some players and fans feel was a conspiracy against the Jets concerning the tarp *purposely* not covering the field, so that it would slow down the speedy Jets. Either way, it was still a winnable game at halftime, with the score deadlocked at 0. But in the second half, it all slipped away from the Jets – into a muddy mess.

Richard Todd would throw a total of five interceptions in the game – including a pick 6 to Dolphins defensive end AJ Duhe in the 4th quarter – which saw the Jets fall one game short of reaching the Super Bowl. You could also pinpoint the loss as the beginning of the end of the "Sack Exchange-era Jets," as it undoubtedly contributed to head coach Walt Michaels' exit (which we've previously discussed).

Final score: Dolphins 14, Jets 0.

5

The Fake Spike Game

"Expect the unexpected" should probably be at the forefront of any athlete's mind participating in a game – *especially* at the pro level. But on November 27, 1994 in a game against the Dolphins at Giants Stadium, the Jets were – to borrow a famous phrase – caught with their pants down.

Going into the game, the Jets were surprisingly right in the thick of things with a 6-5 record. And it looked like they were about to get over the hump and become a legitimate playoff contender once again – with under a minute left in the game, the Jets held a 24-21 lead. The Dolphins got the ball way back on their 16-yard line, with 2:34 left on the clock. One tiny problem…

Dan Marino was Miami's QB.

The eventual Hall of Famer methodically led his team down field – winding up at the Jets' 8-yard line with the clock moving. The Dolphins had one more timeout up their sleeve, so they lined up and Marino motioned that he was going to spike the ball.

"Expect the unexpected," right?

The QB caught the Jets off-guard by firing the ball to WR Mark Ingram in the end zone for a TD (beating then-Jets rookie CB Aaron Glenn) with only 22 seconds left.

After suffering such a devastating loss (which is now universally referred to as "the Fake Spike Game"), the Jets never recovered that season – losing the rest of the games to finish at a disappointing 6-10, and ultimately, costing rookie Jets HC Pete Carroll his job (and would be replaced by – *gasp* – Rich Kotite).

Final score: Dolphins 28, Jets 24.

4

A Brutal Hit
Uncorks a Dynasty

When linebacker Mo Lewis *creamed* Patriots quarterback Drew
Bledsoe on September 23, 2001 (at the 5:03 mark in the 4th quarter,
in the second game of the season) – as Bledsoe was on the run and
trying to get out of bounds – it appeared to serve as a crucial play
in what would turn out to be an important Jets victory.

After all, it obviously affected the Pats' star QB – who despite
returning for the next series in the game, would then be taken out
(Bledsoe was later diagnosed with internal bleeding from the hit).
Plus, this was the Jets' first game back after 9/11 (after a loss to the
Colts in the opening week, 45-24), was a victory against a
divisional opponent, and also, "showed" coach Bill Belichick that
he made a major error snubbing the Jets for the Pats. True?

Untrue.

The Pats' back-up QB was a then-unknown 24-year-old chap by
the name of *Tom Brady*, who then became the Pats' starting QB. I
think you know what happened from there…

Final score: Jets 10, Patriots 3.

3

An All-Time Jet Great Mysteriously Vanishes

Jets QB Flash Gordon was coming off one of his finest seasons ever…and then vanished without a trace. On a peculiarly weathered day in 1980 (which saw planet Earth hit hard by hot hail, earthquakes, hurricanes, typhoons, tornadoes, meteor storms, volcanos erupting, and a solar eclipse, in which the sun completely disappeared in the morning), Gordon was last seen boarding a British short-haul airliner – a de Havilland DH.104 Dove, to be exact – along with New York travel agent, Dale Arden.

Cockpit voice recording transcripts showed that one of the two pilots remarked, "I sure hope Flash Gordon had a great vacation, he's going to have to work hard to top last season," and that they were experiencing some "Clear air turbulence," before all the aviation frequencies went dead on the plane. The aircraft apparently crash-landed into a greenhouse adjacent to the laboratory of controversial scientist Dr. Hans Zarkov, but mysteriously, the bodies of the two pilots were never found (although evidence shows that they were probably ejected through the front window of the plane mid-flight), while the whereabouts of Gordon, Arden, and Zarkov remain unknown.

Although it did appear as though a small rocket ship (that Zarkov possibly constructed himself) lifted off from the scientist's laboratory – as its glass ceiling was found mostly shattered – the ship's destination and location remain unknown. Also revealed at the scene was the body of Munson (Dr. Zarkov's assistant) – who was apparently accidentally crushed to death by the plane during its unexpected landing – as well as a green Jets duffle bag (belonging to Gordon) and an issue of *People Magazine* with Gordon's autograph on the cover, made out to "Buzz" (the son of one of the deceased pilots).

Without question, the Jets sure could have used more heroics from the QB throughout the '80s (perhaps the outcomes of the Mud Bowl and the Marathon by the Lake would have turned out differently). And it's disappointing that the team has yet to retire Gordon's #19 or add his name to their Ring of Honor.

He was a mighty Flash.

2

The Butt Fumble

After Mark Sanchez's first two seasons as the Jets' QB (during which he helped lead the team to two back-to-back AFC Championship Game appearances in 2009 and 2010), it certainly seemed like the team had *finally* found their franchise quarterback – something they had been yearning for since the days of Joe Willie. Hence the press referring to Sanchez at the time as "Sanchize."

But after those first two seasons, the level of Sanchez's play degenerated. So much so, that while looking back at his career today, rather than being best remembered for the accomplishments of his first two seasons, he will probably forever be best known for faceplanting into a teammate's toches on national TV.

Of course, I'm talking about…THE BUTT FUMBLE.

November 22, 2012 happened to be Thanksgiving, and the Jets faced off against their archrival, the Patriots, on national TV that evening. Going into the contest, the Jets were mired in a bad habit that season of winning a game, losing a few games…winning a game, losing a few games – resulting in a subpar 4-6 record. Could a convincing win over the Pats put the Jets back on track?

Maybe. But of course, they didn't beat the Pats. Actually, the Pats *annihilated* the Jets. In fact, things were so bad that in the closing seconds of the first half, the Jets finally managed to score their first points – a field goal – which made the score 35-3!

But when the infamous play occurred – at 9:07 of the 2nd quarter – the Jets were still in the game (down 14-0). So, a step-by-step re-examination of what it takes to construct a Butt Fumble would consist of the following elements:

It all started with a broken play in which Sanchez was looking to hand the ball off to fullback Lex Hilliard. Trying to make something out of nothing, it appeared as though Sanchez panicked and tried to run the ball himself…but instead, opted to run directly into the backside of guard Brandon Moore. And his face met Moore's ass with such force that Sanchez immediately fell on his back (lucky he didn't knock himself out after his head hit the turf) and fumbled the ball – before ultimately admitting defeat and/or shame by rolling over on his stomach and apparently trying to bury his face in the unforgiving ground. Pats safety Steve Gregory scooped up the suddenly unclaimed ball at about the 32-yard line, and promptly returned it for a touchdown.

From that point on, it was clear that the Jets would lose, and lose they did. While watching a replay of the Butt Fumble shortly after its birth, TV sportscaster Cris Collinsworth admitted, "I have never seen this before in my life."

Neither have I, Cris. And hopefully, I will never see a play like that again.

Ever.

Final score: Patriots 49, Jets 19.

And the winner is ...

1

HC of the NYJ

The history of the Jets is shrouded in countless "What if's?" – as in, "What if the field was properly covered by a tarp prior to the AFC Championship Game in Miami?" "What if Aaron Glenn adequately covered Mark Ingram and prevented the 'fake spike TD'?" "What if Vinny Testaverde didn't rupture his Achilles tendon in 1999?" Etcetera, etcetera, etcetera. And the top "What if?" has to be, "What if Bill Belichick didn't bolt from the Jets in 2000 for the Patriots?"

The story goes that once Bill Parcells declined continuing on as the Jets' head coach shortly after the 1999 season wrapped up, Belichick was next in line. Instead, on January 4, 2000, a press conference was held in which Belichick announced that he was not accepting the position, and was in fact, *leaving* the team – and read the following statement aloud:

"Due to the various uncertainties surrounding my position as it relates to the team's new ownership, I've decided to resign as the head coach of the New York Jets. I've given this decision very careful consideration. I would like to wish the entire New York Jets organization, the players, the coaching staff and the new ownership the very best of luck for a prosperous future."

The full text was published the following day in the *New York Post*, in which it was discovered that Belichick had merely jotted down "HC of the NYJ" rather than writing out all the words (on either a napkin or a piece of paper, both have been reported over the years)

– which instantly became a lighthearted catchphrase amongst Jets fans. Either way, the turn of events was shocking. The Jets' then-linebacker coach, Al Groh, was up next to accept the head coaching job of the Jets on January 23rd (with Woody Johnson being announced as the franchise's new owner on January 11th).

Eyebrows were certainly raised when it became known that the Patriots sought to hire Belichick as their head coach – leading many to believe that there was alleged wheeling and dealing going on behind the scenes. And since Parcells and the Jets claimed that Belichick was still under contract with them, they demanded compensation.

NFL commissioner Paul Tagliabue sided with the Jets concerning this matter, and the Pats had to give up their first round draft pick in 2000 in order to hire Belichick (which they made official on January 27th via a press conference). And it also became clear *why* Belichick left the Jets for the Pats – Pats owner Robert Kraft was willing to give him almost total control (making him the team's GM, as well). Whereas, if he stayed with the Jets, Parcells would still be over him (as GM).

What many forget – since Belichick's Pats would become an NFL dynasty – is that the team was not very good early on with Belichick at the helm, going just 5-11 in 2000. And things didn't look better at the start of 2001, as the Pats began 0-2. But it was during the second loss that one of the "luckiest injuries" in the history of pro sports occurred (which you've already read about in entry #4), which led to Tom Brady becoming, well...*Tom Brady*.

From the time that Belichick became the Pats' HC to this book's release, his team has won 6 Super Bowls, 9 AFC titles, and 17 division championships (compared to the Jets 0 Super Bowls, 0 AFC titles, and 1 division championship), and is *still* the Pats' HC (which in that same time frame, the Jets have employed 7 different HC's).

"What if?", *indeed*.

THE LIST

100. The Jets Killed Carl
99. A Skirmish at Studio 54
98. Joe Namath…Actor?
97. SNY Lets Ray Lucas Go
96. Chad's Awkward Comments to the Press
95. A Roughed Up Reporter
94. Rex Ryan's Tattoo
93. What a Thrilling Comeback Victory…Oops, Spoke Too Soon
92. A Touchdown Celebration That Stunk
91. Hiring an Offensive Coordinator With Little Offensive Coordinating Experience
90. NFL Player Strikes Ground 2 Jets Seasons
89. Once Upon a Time, Playing In a Stadium Not Designed for Football
88. Lou Holtz's Not Quite Full Season's Fight Song
87. Leon's Secret to Success
86. Well, At Least We Have Jay Fiedler as a Back-up QB…Oh Wait, We Don't
85. Titans Throwback Helmets/Uniforms Rather Than '78-'97 Jets Helmets/Uniforms
84. Washington Jetskins
83. Tebow Time
82. The Jamal Adams Saga
81. The Jets' Worst Regular Season Loss Ever?
80. Billy "White Shoes" Johnson
79. Shouldn't They Be Called the New Jersey Jets?
78. Free Agency and Draft Navigator Gets Fired a Few Weeks Later
77. A Mid-Game Weiner
76. De-feet
75. Author Rex
74. Author Keyshawn
73. Replay Officials Suffer a Brain Fart
72. West Side Stadium

71. Awakening Sleeping Giants
70. Hissy Fit In the Huddle
69. Let's Hire My Son-in-Law as My Replacement
68. Gastineau's Sack Dance Spawns Excessive Celebrations
67. The Human Wall
66. Beating This Winless Team Should Be a Breeze
65. Matt Robinson's Sore Thumb
64. Giving the Sanchize an Extension
63. Re-signing Fitz
62. The Erosion of Revis Island
61. Signing a Bad Newz QB
60. Gee, Broadway Joe Is Getting Injured a Lot These Days. Shouldn't We Find a Serviceable Back-up QB? *Nah.*
59. The Last Jets Game at Shea
58. Goodbye Chad, Hello Brett
57. Sexual Harassment in the Workplace (Part I)
56. Sexual Harassment in the Workplace (Part II)
55. Sexual Harassment in the Workplace (Part III)
54. Gregg Williams' Incomprehensible Play Call
53. "I'm seeing ghosts"
52. "I want to kiss you"
51. Broadway Joe "Retires"
50. The Fireman "Retires"
49. Goodbye USA, Hello UK
48. Jawbreaker
47. Putting Sanchez in a Meaningless Pre-Season Game
46. Not Going to Ray Lucas Sooner in 1999
45. No More Giving Him the Damn Ball
44. Firing Pete Carroll After One Season
43. The Idzik 12
42. All They Need to Do Is Beat the Lions to Get Into the Playoffs
41. All They Need to Do Is Beat the Bills to Get Into the Playoffs
40. Ken, Al, and Freeman's Playoff Swan Song
39. The Last Jets Playoff Game at Shea
38. Should We Secure the #1 Pick? No. We Should Not.
37. The Final 5 of '86
36. Free Agent Failures

OTHER BOOKS BY GREG PRATO

Sports:
Sack Exchange: The Definitive Oral History of the 1980s New York Jets

Dynasty: The Oral History of the New York Islanders, 1972-1984

Just Out of Reach: The 1980s New York Yankees

The Seventh Year Stretch: New York Mets, 1977-1983

Music:
A Devil on One Shoulder and an Angel on the Other: The Story of Shannon Hoon and Blind Melon

Touched by Magic: The Tommy Bolin Story

Grunge Is Dead: The Oral History of Seattle Rock Music

No Schlock...Just Rock! (A Journalistic Journey: 2003-2008)

MTV Ruled the World: The Early Years of Music Video

The Eric Carr Story

Too High to Die: Meet the Meat Puppets

The Faith No More & Mr. Bungle Companion

Overlooked/Underappreciated: 354 Recordings That Demand Your Attention

Over the Electric Grapevine: Insight into Primus and the World of Les Claypool

Punk! Hardcore! Reggae! PMA! Bad Brains!

Iron Maiden: '80 '81

Survival of the Fittest: Heavy Metal in the 1990s

Scott Weiland: Memories of a Rock Star

German Metal Machine: Scorpions in the '70s

The Other Side of Rainbow

Shredders!: The Oral History of Speed Guitar (And More)

The Yacht Rock Book: The Oral History of the Soft, Smooth Sounds of the 60s, 70s, and 80s

100 Things Pearl Jam Fans Should Know & Do Before They Die

The 100 Greatest Rock Bassists

Long Live Queen: Rock Royalty Discuss Freddie, Brian, John & Roger

King's X: The Oral History

Facts on Tracks: Stories Behind 100 Rock Classics

Dark Black and Blue: The Soundgarden Story

Take It Off: Kiss Truly Unmasked

A Rockin' Rollin' Man: Bon Scott Remembered

Avatar of the Electric Guitar: The Genius of Jimi Hendrix

BONZO: 30 Rock Drummers Remember the Legendary John Bonham

John Winston Ono Lennon

Made in the USA
Columbia, SC
15 November 2021

49022307R00100